The Flip of a Coin
and Other Short Stories

Dans la même collection

Lire en anglais

Thirteen Modern English and American Short Stories
Seven American Short Stories
Nine English Short Stories
Roald Dahl : Someone Like You and Other
Short Stories
Roald Dahl : The Hitch-Hiker and Other
Short Stories
Somerset Maugham : The Escape and Other Short
Stories
F. Scott Fitzgerald : Pat Hobby and Orson Welles
and Other Short Stories
Ray Bradbury : Kaleidoscope and Other
Short Stories

Lire en allemand

Moderne Erzählungen
Deutsche Kurzgeschichten
Zwanzig Kurzgeschichten des 20. Jahrhunderts

Lire en espagnol

Cuentos selectos
Jorge Luis Borges : La Intrusa y otros cuentos
(à paraître)

LIRE EN ANGLAIS
Collection dirigée par Henri Yvinec

Somerset Maugham

The Flip of a Coin
and
Other Short Stories

Choix et annotations par William B. Barrie M.A. - M. ès L.
Maître de Conférences à l'Université de Paris VII
Lecturer British Institute in Paris - University of London

Enregistrement sur cassette

Le Livre de Poche

Du même auteur

Dictionnaire de l'anglais d'aujourd'hui, 1982, en collaboration (Édition Garnier et France-Loisirs)

Which and How — Vocabulaire structural, 1968, Didier

La collection "Les Langues Modernes" n'a pas de lien avec l'A.P.L.V. et les ouvrages qu'elle publie le sont sous sa seule responsabilité.

Sommaire

Abbreviations

adj adjective
adv adverb
Am American
aux *verbe auxiliaire*
cf. confer (see)
e.g. for example
emph emphatic
excl exclamative
fam familiar
fig figurative
fml formal
idiom idiomatic
i.e. id est *(c'est-à-dire)*
lit literary
n noun
pej pejorative
plur plural
prep preposition
qqch. *quelque chose*
qqn. *quelqu'un*
sb somebody, someone
sing singular
sl slang
sth something
tps *temps du verbe*
U uncountable singular noun
v verb
= synonym
≠ antonym
Ø zero article or zero relative pronoun

Tout naturellement, après quelques années d'étude d'une langue étrangère, naît l'envie de découvrir sa littérature. Mais, par ailleurs, le vocabulaire dont on dispose est souvent insuffisant. La perspective de recherches lexicales multipliées chez le lecteur isolé, la présentation fastidieuse du vocabulaire, pour le professeur, sont autant d'obstacles redoutables. C'est pour tenter de les aplanir que nous proposons cette nouvelle collection.

Celle-ci constitue une étape vers la lecture autonome, sans dictionnaire ni traduction, grâce à des notes facilement repérables. S'agissant des élèves de lycée, les ouvrages de cette collection seront un précieux instrument pédagogique pour les enseignants en langues étrangères puisque les recommandations pédagogiques officielles (Bulletin officiel de l'Éducation nationale du 9 juillet 1987) les invitent à "faire de l'entraînement à la lecture individuelle une activité régulière" qui pourra aller jusqu'à une heure hebdomadaire. Ces recueils de textes devraient ainsi servir de complément à l'étude de la civilisation.

Le lecteur trouvera donc :

En page de gauche

Des textes contemporains choisis pour leur intérêt littéraire et la qualité de leur langue.

En page de droite

Des notes juxtalinéaires rédigées dans la langue du texte, qui aident le lecteur à

Comprendre

Tous les mots et expressions difficiles contenus dans la ligne de gauche sont reproduits en caractères gras et expliqués dans le contexte.

Observer

Des notes d'observation de la langue soulignent le caractère idiomatique de certaines tournures ou constructions.

Apprendre

Dans un but d'enrichissement lexical, certaines notes proposent enfin des synonymes, des antonymes, des expressions faisant appel aux mots qui figurent dans le texte.

Grammaire au fil des nouvelles

Chaque nouvelle est suivie de phrases de thème inspirées du texte avec références à celui-ci pour le corrigé. En les traduisant le lecteur, mis sur la voie par des italiques et/ou des amorces d'explication, révise les structures rebelles les plus courantes ; cette petite "grammaire en contexte" est fondée sur la fréquence des erreurs.

Vocabulaire

En fin de volume, une liste d'un millier de mots contenus dans les nouvelles, suivis de leur traduction, comporte, entre autres, les verbes irréguliers et les mots qui n'ont pas été annotés faute de place ou parce que leur sens était évident dans le contexte. Grâce à ce lexique on pourra, en dernier recours, procéder à quelques vérifications ou faire un bilan des mots retenus au cours des lectures.

A few more words about the author

If you have read *The Escape and Other Short Stories,* which was the first volume of stories by W. Somerset Maugham in this series, you will know that he was born on 25 January 1874 in the building of the British Embassy in Paris, as was the rule at that time, in order to have British nationality, that he died on 16 December 1965 in his *Villa Mauresque* at Saint-Jean-Cap-Ferrat. At his own request, his ashes were buried on 22 December at the King's School, Canterbury —surely a curious case of mixed motivations on the part of Maugham, for we remember how he had detested that establishment when he was a schoolboy there.

You will also know that his life was difficult to start with, both professionally and personally until he suddenly became famous with a play at the age of just over thirty. From then on he was successful in the sense that he was well-known, rich, free to do as he wished. Yet it can hardly be said he was a happy man. Rather he was a man obsessed by a search for the happiness that always seemed to elude him. In the stories included in this volume *The Happy Man* and *The Lotus Eater* we find two examples of this preoccupation.

This constant dissatisfaction, this sense of frustration, may to some extent be explained by his childhood difficulties. He had a passion for his mother, and perhaps a certain fear of his father, who worked long hours and had little time to spend with his son. Maugham once wrote: "My father was a stranger to me." He also recounted that his parents were known as "Beauty and the Beast" and that Lady Anglesey once told him that she had asked his mother why she had married such an ugly man. She had received the answer: "He never hurts my feelings."

And indeed, Edith Mary Snell Maugham's son, who was to live a life full of honours, always seemed to be afraid that someone might hurt his feelings. Of course, the early death of his parents could not fail to affect a boy as young and as sensitive as he was.

9

After all, he was only eight years old when his mother died, and ten at his father's death.

In his autobiography, *The Summing Up*, Maugham describes how his feelings had been hurt by his mother's death: "When I was a small boy I used to dream night after night that my life at school was a dream and that I should wake to find myself at home again with my mother."

In order to protect his feelings from being further hurt Maugham learned how to use a defensive armour, and disciplined himself to show only those features of himself that he chose to reveal. To find emotion, personal or otherwise, in a Maugham short story or novel one has to look very hard under the surface, to read between the lines. It is perhaps in his longer short stories that, almost accidentally, his own feelings or opinions show up most clearly —though always indirectly.

With *Gigolo and Gigolette*, which we have included in this volume, we become emotionally involved in the circus people, who know very well how precarious any artistic success is, and how lonely. The hero of *The Lotus Eater* typifies the quest for happiness with a pathos that stirs us, despite the cool, objective style that Maugham invariably uses. *The Alien Corn* gives us a superficially ironical but profoundly affectionate, tender portrait of a Jewish family who obviously symbolize the eternal "outsiders" among whom Maugham considered himself exiled.

For, in spite of his literary successes, he always seems to have felt that he was someone who never really "belonged" anywhere —unlike his elder brothers who were will integrated inside the established social order. He had been unhappy at school, where he detested sports, and his university studies had been at Heidelberg and London, instead of Oxford or Cambridge. The feeling continued even much later in life, when everyone who was anyone came to see him, either in London or at the *Villa Mauresque*. He was, in fact, on visiting terms with almost all the famous people of his time: Winston Churchill, Grace Kelly, Adlai Stevenson, Lord Beaverbrook, the Duke and Duchess of Windsor, the Aga

Khan, Ian Fleming, Max Beerbohm, Rudyard Kipling, H.G. Wells, Arnold Bennet, Aldous Huxley, Jean Cocteau, Noel Coward, John Le Carré, to mention only a few.

He sought happiness in the world of art, yet somehow seemed to remain frustrated. He once exclaimed: "Beauty is a bore!" It is true that he then went on to explain what exactly he meant. After the first few seconds or minutes of being dazzled we are forced to find other occupations than the pure contemplation of an object of beauty. Critics of art and literature, he claimed, do not discuss beauty. They analyse style, technique, history, psychology, establish comparisons with other works of art, and so forth. But this is an intellectual activity that is only very indirectly connected with beauty, if at all.

Maugham was never the type of writer who forgets or neglects the material pleasures of life. He did find a great deal of happiness in writing, and commented: "I have never been so happy or so much at ease as when, seated at my table, from my pen flowed word after word", but the sentence ends significantly:... "until the luncheon gong forced me to put an end to the day's work." Meal times were sacred! Indeed, one of the attractions of the *Villa Mauresque* was its *cuisine*.

He had little patience with the self-important "inspired" writers, endowed with a cultural mission and a solid belief in their own genius. He once flew into a fury when invited to make a financial contribution in favour of Max Beerbohm, with whom he had a love-hate relationship and who was then living on the Italian Riviera, waiting for inspiration. Maugham's inspiration consisted in sitting down regularly at his desk every morning to write, and Max could damn well do the same!

Which did not mean that Maugham could not be generous in helping other writers financially. He often was. But he preferred to help those who also helped themselves, and he was irritated more than once at the attitude of critics towards certain fellow-writers about whom it could be said that the less they wrote the greater was their reputation.

11

During his lifetime, despite his enormous productivity and great popularity, Somerset Maugham was never acclaimed as a major literary figure. He was chiefly regarded as a good artisan, but no genius. In *The Summing Up* he comments not without a certain bitterness: "In my twenties the critics said I was brutal, in my thirties they said I was flippant, in my forties they said I was cynical, in my fifties they said I was competent, and now in my sixties they say I am superficial."

Maybe his fear of having his feelings hurt prevented him from giving his full measure, for this apparent superficiality may well have been the armour that the child Maugham developed to protect him from a world he felt to be hostile. For many years Maugham was unwilling to admit and assume his homosexuality in such a world. In his writing he practised the same self-effacement. He presented the bare facts and left it to the reader to draw his own conclusions and make his own judgements. It was and always will be up to the reader to perceive the sensibility beneath the smooth, urbane style.

No writer is indispensable, but the reading world would be poorer and sadder without William Somerset Maugham. Let us give H.G. Wells the last word. When he sent Maugham one of his own books as a Christmas present in 1934 he dedicated it as follows: "*To Willie, God bless him.*"

The Flip of a Coin

The character of James Bond, created by Ian Fleming, popularized the intelligence agent who is a kind of superman, having at his disposal a whole armoury of sophisticated gadgets, particularly in the films adapted from the novels.

On the other hand, writers such as Raymond Postgate, with *The Ledger is Kept* and later John Le Carré in *The Spy Who Came in from the Cold* and other espionage stories, chose to describe a different and more true-to-life type of intelligence agent — one who lived an apparently ordinary life, since his survival depended on making himself invisible — an agent who was often disillusioned, knowing he could be directed, manœuvred and even sacrificed like a pawn in a game of chess by cynical superiors.

All these writers had a precursor in the person of Somerset Maugham, who had been a member of the Intelligence Service in the 1914-1918 World War. From his own experience he knew the reality of day-to-day espionage — most of the time a monotonous rather then a heroic existence, made up of routine investigations and boring burocratic work, with the discipline of a strict hierarchy to be respected.

Yet it remains true that some very hard decisions may have to be taken occasionally, especially in wartime, that involve the lives of many other men. Who is to take these decisions? On what basis? Could it be that some of these decisions simply depend on chance, on the flip of a coin?

It was high time. Snow had fallen in the morning, but now the sky was clear and Ashenden, with a glance at the frosty stars, stepped out quickly. He feared that Herbartus, tired of waiting for him, might have gone home. He had at this interview to make a certain decision and the hesitation he felt about it had lurked throughout the evening at the back of his mind like a malaise that had only to become a little more definite to be felt as pain. For Herbartus, indefatigable and determined, had been engaged in the
10 arrangement of a scheme to blow up certain munition factories in Austria. It is not necessary to give here the details of his plan, but it was ingenious and effective; its drawback was that it entailed the death and mutilation of a good many Galician Poles, his fellow countrymen, who were working in the factories in question. He had told Ashenden earlier in the day that everything was ready and he had only to give the word.

"But please do not give it unless it is essential," he said in his precise, somewhat throaty English. "Of course we will
20 not hesitate if it is necessary, but we do not want to sacrifice our own people for nothing."

"When do you want an answer?"

"To-night. We have got someone who is starting for Prague to-morrow morning."

It was then that Ashenden had made the appointment that he was now hurrying to keep.

"You will not be late, will you?" Herbartus had said. "I shall not be able to catch the messenger after midnight."

Ashenden had qualms and he was conscious that it would
30 be a relief if on reaching the hotel he found that Herbartus had left. That would give him a respite. The Germans had blown up factories in the Allied countries and there was no

14

high time: almost late; it's (high) time we left *(note the tense!)* = we had better leave, or we'll be late

frosty: suggestive of freezing temperatures □ **stars** = *étoiles*

interview: *here* = meeting

had lurked: had been hiding in a menacing way □ **throughout**: during □ **at the back of his mind**: in his semi-consciousness

felt *(feel, felt, felt)* perceived

indefatigable: untiring □ **engaged in**: busy on, involved in, concerned with □ **scheme**: project, plan □ **blow up**: explode □

munition factories: ammunition works □ **it is not necessary to give** = we need not give □ **ingenious**: skilful; full of ingenuity, skill

drawback: disadvantage □ **entailed**: involved, implied

a good many: very many □ **fellow countrymen**: compatriots i.e. people belonging to the same country; cf. *fellow pupils, fellow students, fellow doctors...* who belong to the same category

give the word: say the word, give the order

unless it is essential: if it is not absolutely necessary

throaty: guttural, hoarse

sacrifice: make the sacrifice of

for nothing: to no purpose, to no end, if it does no good

want an answer: want (me to give you) an answer

starting for: leaving for

appointment: arrangement to meet someone

hurrying: rushing; in a hurry; in a rush □ **keep** *(kept, kept)*

be late ≠ be on time, be punctual

catch *(caught, caught)*: contact

qualms: doubts, scruples

relief: weight off his conscience □ **on reaching**: when he got to

left *(leave, left, left)*: gone away □ **respite**: rest from stress

Allied countries: when one country is the ally of another

reason why they should not be served in the same manner. It was a legitimate act of war. It not only hindered the manufacture of arms and munitions, but also shook the morale of the non-combatants. It was not of course a thing that the big-wigs cared to have anything to do with. Though ready enough to profit by the activities of obscure agents of whom they had never heard, they shut their eyes to dirty work so that they could put their clean hands on their hearts and congratulate themselves that they had never done
10 anything that was unbecoming to men of honour. Ashenden thought with cynical humour of an incident in his relations with R. He had been approached with an offer that he thought it his duty to put before his chief.

"By the way", he said to him as casually as possible, "I've got a sportsman who's willing to assassinate King B. for five thousand pounds."

King B. was the ruler of a Balkan state which was on the verge through his influence of declaring war against the Allies, and it was evident that his disappearance from the
20 scene would be extremely useful. His successor's sympathies were indefinite and it might be possible to persuade him to keep his country neutral. Ashenden saw from R.'s quick, intent look that he was perfectly aware of the situation. But he frowned sulkily.

"Well, what of it?"

"I told him I'd transmit his offer. I believe he's perfectly genuine. He's pro-Ally and he thinks it would about bust his country if it went in on the side of the Germans."

"What's he want five thousand pounds for, then?"
30 "It's a risk and if he does the Allies a good turn he doesn't see why he shouldn't get something out of it."

R. shook his head energetically.

served: treated; it would serve them right

war: warfare *(= guerre)* □ **hindered**: obstructed, was an obstacle to □ **arms**: (singular = *a weapon*) □ **shook**: perturbed

morale: spirit ≠ *moral* (of a story) ≠ *morals* = principles

big-wigs: chiefs □ **cared**: liked □ **have... do with**: be involved in

profit by: benefit from

of... heard: unknown to them □ **shut their eyes**: turned a blind eye □ **dirty work**: unpleasant activities (that dirty your hands)

congratulate... done: congratulate themselves *on* never doing

unbecoming: unworthy (of them); which did not become them

cynical: a *cynic* is *cynical* because of his *cynicism*

he had been approached: sb had come to see him (with an offer)

duty: responsiblity, job □ **put before**: submit (for approval) to

by the way: incidentally □ **casually**: informally, indifferently

sportsman: adventurous fellow □ **willing**: ready ≠ unwilling, reluctant

ruler: head; he ruled the state □ **on the verge... of declaring**: on the point of declaring, about to declare □ **through**: thanks to

his disappearance: the possibility of him (his) disappearing

sympathies: inclinations (towards one country or the other)

it might... persuade: he might be persuaded

neutral: neither on one side or the other

intent: attentive □ **aware**: conscious; consciousness, awareness

frowned: gave a sign of disapproval with his eyebrows □ **sulkily**: disapprovingly □ **What of it?**: What does it matter? So what? *(fam)*

transmit: hand on (to someone else)

genuine: authentic, sincere, in good faith □ **about bust**: nearly burst, ruined □ **went in**: entered (the war)

What's he want... for: what does he want... for; why does he want...

does the Allies a good turn: renders the Allies a good service

why he shouldn't: note *should* after *why*

energetically: with energy, vigorously, briskly

"It's not the kind of thing we can have anything to do with. We don't wage war by those methods. We leave them to the Germans. Damn it all, we are gentlemen."

Ashenden did not reply, but watched R. with attention. There was in his eyes the curious reddish light that they sometimes had and that gave them so sinister an expression. He had always a slight tendency to squint and now he was quite definitely cross-eyed.

"You ought to know better than to put up a proposition
10 like that to me. Why didn't you knock the man down when he made it?"

"I didn't think I could," said Ashenden. "He was bigger than I. Besides, it never occurred to me. He was very civil and obliging."

"Of course it would be a damned good thing for the Allies if King B. were out of the way. I admit that. But between that and countenancing his assassination there's all the difference between black and white. If the man were a patriot I should have thought he'd have gone straight ahead
20 and done what he thought right regardless."

"He may be thinking of his widow," said Ashenden.

"Anyhow, it's not a matter I'm prepared to discuss. Different people look at things in different ways and if anyone thought he was helping the Allies by taking on his own shoulders a heavy responsibility that's of course entirely his look-out."

It took Ashenden a moment to see what his chief meant. Then he smiled thinly.

"Don't think I'm going to pay the fellow five thousand
30 pounds out of my own pocket. Not a chance."

"I don't think anything of the kind and you know I don't,

thing we can... with : project (that) we can be implicated (involved) in □ **wage war** : make war, warfare □ **leave** *(left, left)*
damn it all : hell, to hell, for heaven's sake, in heaven's name
with attention : attentively, intently, closely
curious : strange, odd □ **reddish** : red-tinged
so sinister an expression : such a sinister expression
had... a slight tendency to squint : tended to have a slight strabism
was... cross-eyed : his eyes did not look in the same direction
put up a proposition : make a proposal, submit a project
like that : such as that □ **knock the man down** : hit him (so that he fell to the ground)
I didn't think I could : I thought it wasn't possible
it... occurred to me : it never came into my mind □ **civil** : polite
obliging : ready to oblige, to render services, to do a favour
damned good : very, extremely good
if King B. were out of the way : if someone got rid of King B.
countenancing : approving of ; giving approval for

gone straight ahead : carried out his project without hesitating
thought right : considered (as being) right □ **regardless** : in spite of all obstacles □ **widow** : his wife after his death
matter : question, problem, affair □ **prepared** : willing, ready
look at things : consider, regard things
taking on his own shoulders : assuming alone, by himself

entirely his look-out : his own responsibility
it took... a moment : (Ashenden) took (needed) a moment □ **meant** : wanted him to understand □ **thinly** : ironically ≠ broadly
fellow : man chap ; *(Am)* guy
out of my own pocket : of my own money ; I don't want to be out of pocket □ **not a chance** : that will never happen

19

and I shall be obliged if you won't exercise your very deficient sense of humour on me."

Ashenden shrugged his shoulders; and now, recalling the conversation, he shrugged them again. They were all like that. They desired the end, but hesitated at the means. They were willing to take advantage of an accomplished fact, but wanted to shift on to someone else the responsibility of bringing it about.

Ashenden entered the café of the Hotel de Paris and saw Herbartus seated at a table facing the door. He gave the little gasp that is forced from you when you dive into water that is colder than you expected. There was no escape. He must make the decision. Herbartus was drinking a glass of tea. His heavy, clean-shaven face lit up when he saw Ashenden and he stretched out a large, hairy hand. He was a big, dark fellow, of a powerful build, with fierce black eyes. Everything about him suggested a massive strength. He was hampered by no scruples, and since he was disinterested he was ruthless.

"Well, how did your dinner go off?" he asked as Ashenden sat down. "Did you say anything to the ambassador about our project?"

"No."

"I think you were wise. It is best to leave those sort of people out of serious matters."

Ashenden looked at Herbartus for a minute reflectively. His face bore a singular expression and he sat warily like a tiger about to spring.

"Have you ever read Balzac's *Père Goriot*?" asked Ashenden suddenly.

"Twenty years ago, when I was a student."

"Do you remember that conversation between Rastignac

obliged : grateful □ **won't exercise :** are willing not to experiment

shrugged his shoulders : gave a gesture of indifference □ **recalling :** remembering □ **like that :** the same ; they resembled each other
end : result □ **means :** way to achieve an end ; a means towards an end □ **willing :** ready □ **take advantage of :** profit from, benefit from
shift : move, transfer □ **responsibility :** being responsible *for*
bringing it about : achieving it ; getting the result
entered the café : went into the café ; N.B. enter *into* details
seated : sitting □ **facing :** opposite □ **gave... gasp :** breathed in quickly □ **forced from you :** (that) you cannot help (giving) □ **dive :** plunge □ **there was no escape :** there was/were no means of escaping
must make : had to make (N.B. *must* can be invariable in indirect speech) □ **clean-shaven :** with neither beard nor moustache □ **lit up :** brightened (up) □ **stretched out :** extended □ **hairy :** covered with hair □ **build :** body, frame □ **fierce :** savage, frightening, cruel
everything about him : his general appearance □ **massive :** solid
hampered : hindered, inhibited, handicapped □ **no scruples :** (he was) quite unscrupulous □ **ruthless :** without pity, pitiless, remorseless □ **how... go off? :** was (your dinner) successful?
sat down : took a seat
project : plan, scheme

wise : prudent, cautious □ **those sort... :** those kind(s) of people □ **leave... out of serious matters :** exclude... from serious questions
for a minute : note *for* with duration □ **reflectively :** thoughtfully
singular : strange, odd, unusual □ **warily :** distrustfully, cautiously
about to spring : ready to jump, prepared to leap
ever : at any time

read... 20 years ago : it's 20 years since I (last) read it ; I haven't read it for 20 years. Note the tenses

and Vautrin where they discuss the question whether, were you able by a nod to effect the death of a mandarin in China and so bring yourself a colossal fortune, you would give the nod? It was a notion of Rousseau's."

Herbartus's large face coiled itself into a slow, large smile.

"It has nothing to do with the case. You are uneasy at giving an order that will cause the death of a considerable number of people. Is it for your own profit? When a general
10 orders an advance he knows that so and so many men will be killed. It is war."

"What a stupid war!"

"It will give my country freedom."

"What will your country do with it when it gets it?"

Herbartus did not answer. He shrugged his shoulders.

"I warn you that if you do not take this opportunity it may not recur very soon. We cannot send a messenger over the frontier every day of the week."

"Doesn't it make you a little uncomfortable to think of
20 all those men being suddenly blown to smithereens by an explosion? And then it's not only the dead, it's the maimed."

"I don't like it. I said to you that on account of my fellow countrymen who will be sacrificed we should do nothing unless it was worth while. I dot not want those poor fellows to be killed, but if they are I shall not sleep less soundly nor eat my dinner with less appetite. Will you?"

"I suppose not."

"Well, then?"
30 Ashenden thought on a sudden of those sharp-pointed stars on which for a moment his eyes had rested as he walked through the frosty night. It seemed an age since he

22

discuss the question: N.B. direct object = talk *about* the question □
were you able: if you were able □ **nod**: approving sign of the head
so: in that way, by that means
a... of Rousseau's: a (notion) belonging to Rousseau. Cf. a friend
of mine □ **coiled itself into a smile**: changed (like a serpent) into...

nothing to do with the case: no relation to, connection with the
question □ **uneasy**: uncomfortable, ill at ease

so and so many men: (in answer to the question *"How many?"*) a
certain number of men □ **war**: warfare; one country is *at* war *with*
another. Note the prepositions
freedom: liberty
do with it: achieve with (this freedom) □ **gets it**: achieves it
shrugged his shoulders: gave a gesture of indifference
warn you: put you on your guard □ **opportunity**: occasion, chance
recur: occur, happen another time □ **over**: to the other side of

make... uncomfortable: give you doubts, remorse, uneasiness
blown to smithereens: torn to small pieces (by an explosion)
the dead: the men who have died
the maimed: those who are badly injured, crippled for life
on account of: because of □ **fellow-countrymen**: compatriots

worth while: worth (while) doing, worth the sacrifice □ **I do not
want those poor fellows to be killed**: N.B. the infinitive structure
after *want* and verbs with a similar meaning □ **soundly**:
profoundly, deeply, peacefully □ **I suppose not**: I don't think so;
probably not
on a sudden: suddenly □ **sharp-pointed**: with sharp points, spiky
stars = *étoiles* □ **rested**: paused, fixed, alighted
frosty: icy cold, freezing

had sat in the spacious dining-room at the embassy and listened to Sir Herbert Witherspoon's story of his successful, wasted life. Mr. Schäfer's susceptibilities and his own small intrigues, the love of Byring and Rose Auburn: how unimportant; Man, with so short a time between the cradle and the grave, spent his life in foolishness. A trivial creature! The bright stars shone in the cloudless sky.

"I'm tired, I can't think with any clearness."

"I must go in a minute."

10 "Then let's toss for it, shall we?"

"Toss?"

"Yes," said Ashenden, taking a coin out of his pocket. "If it comes down heads tell your man to go ahead and if it comes down tails tell him to do nothing."

"Very well."

Ashenden balanced the coin on his thumb-nail and flicked it neatly into the air. They watched it spin and when it fell back on the table Ashenden put his hand over it. They both leaned forward to look as Ashenden very slowly

20 withdrew his hand. Herbartus drew a deep breath.

"Well, that's that," said Ashenden.

spacious: roomy □ **embassy**: the ambassador's residence

wasted: unprofitable; he had wasted his life, his time

so short a time: such a short time □ **cradle**: baby's bed
grave: tomb □ **trivial**: unimportant, futile
shone *(shine, shone, shone)*: were brilliant; sparkled □ **cloudless**: without a cloud, perfectly clear, limpid
in a minute: very soon
toss for it: throw (a coin into the air) to decide the question □ **let's... shall we?** N.B. the question tag with *shall*
coin: piece of money □ **if it comes down heads**: if the head is visible when the coin falls down again □ **go ahead**: do it
tails: the other side of the coin

balanced: held (the coin) in equilibrium □ **thumb-nail** = *ongle du pouce* □ **flicked**: tossed it lightly □ **neatly**: skilfully □ **spin**: revolve
put his hand over it: covered it with his hand
leaned forward: bent forward
withdrew: pulled back □ **drew** *(draw, drew, drawn)* **a deep breath**: breathed in deeply □ **that's that**: that's settled, that settles that

Grammaire au fil des nouvelles

Traduisez les phrases suivantes inspirées du texte (le premier chiffre renvoie à la page, les suivants aux lignes).

Il craignait que Hebertus ne soit rentré chez lui (ce degré de probabilité = *may? might? must?* 14 - 3,4).

Maintenant il devait prendre une certaine décision (c'est une obligation, donc *must? had to? should?* 14 - 4,5).

Ne donnez pas l'ordre à moins que cela ne soit essentiel (unless = if...not, 14 - 18).

Il n'y avait pas de raison qu'on ne leur rendît pas la pareille (*no reason for* ...ou bien *no reason why*... 16 - 1).

Il était suffisamment enclin à tirer profit des activités d'agents obscurs (position de *enough*, 16 - 6).

Les "gros bonnets" ne tenaient pas à s'en mêler (I never care to have anything to do with big-wigs... 16 - 5).

Sa disparition de la scène politique serait extrêmement utile aux Alliés (*stage* ou *scene*? 16 - 19,20).

Vous devriez savoir qu'il vaut mieux ne pas me faire une telle proposition (les convenances... *must? ought to?* 18 - 9).

Il n'y avait aucune issue. Il devait prendre la décision (*must* est-il possible dans ce discours indirect libre? 20 - 12).

Vous êtes gêné à la pensée d'avoir à donner un tel ordre (*uneasy at* + *le gérondif* pourrait être un moyen économique... 22 - 6).

Quelle guerre stupide (*such* et *what* seront suivis de Ø ou de *a*? nom indénombrable ou dénombrable? 22 - 11)**!**

Cette occasion pourrait ne pas se représenter de sitôt (une éventualité... quel auxiliaire modal? 22 - 16).

Ne faites rien à moins que cela n'en vaille la peine (unless = if...not 22 - 25).

Il ne voulait pas que ces pauvres types soient tués (proposition infinitive après un verbe coercitif, 22 - 25,26).

Il lui semblait qu'une éternité s'était écoulée depuis qu'il se trouvait assis dans l'ambassade (we haven't met for an age = it's an age since we (last) met... 22 - 32).

Il prit une pièce de monnaie dans sa poche (mouvement d'éloignement, donc : *take to? take from?* 24 - 12).

Raw Material

Like all authors, Somerset Maugham was continually on the look-out for raw material for his writing. Although imagination is the essential for a novelist, he needs to find some support for his characters by observing how things happen and how people behave in real life, and Somerset Maugham was no exception to the rule. It was even one of the reasons why he liked travelling so much.

Here we start out on our journey at Haiphong, calling at Hong-Kong, then via Shanghai to Peking before returning to the United States. Plenty of time for observation — if there is anyone worth observing! As luck would have it, there are on board two American gentlemen who look too good to be true. In fact, public rumour has it that they are two notorious cardsharpers travelling incognito. But how to find a way into their confidence? How to persuade them to tell some of the secrets of their profession — and the underlying mentality?

I have long had in mind a novel in which a card-sharper was the principal character; and, going up and down the world, I have kept my eyes open for members of this profession. Because the idea is prevalent that it is a slightly dishonourable one the persons who follow it do not openly acknowledge the fact. Their reticence is such that it is often not till you have become quite closely acquainted with them, or even have played cards with them two or three times, that you discover in what fashion they earn their
10 living. But even then they have a disinclination to enlarge upon the mysteries of their craft. They have a weakness for passing themselves off for cavalrymen, commercial agents, or landed proprietors. This snobbish attitude makes them the most difficult class in the world for the novelist to study. It has been my good fortune to meet a number of these gentlemen, and though I have found them affable, obliging, and debonair, I have no sooner hinted, however discreetly, at my curiosity (after all purely professional) in the technique of their calling than they have grown shy and
20 uncommunicative. An airy reference on my part to stacking the cards has made them assume immediately the appearance of a clam. I am not easily discouraged, and learning by experience that I could hope for no good results from a direct method, I have adopted the oblique. I have been childlike with them and bland. I have found that they gave me their attention and even their sympathy. Though they confessed honestly that they had never read a word I had written they were interested by the fact that I was a writer. I suppose they felt obscurely that I too followed a
30 calling that the Philistine regarded without indulgence. But I have been forced to gather my facts by a bold surmise. It has needed patience and industry.

28

I have long had in mind : I have been planning for a long time
novel = *roman* □ **card-sharper :** sby who cheats at cards □ **going
up and down the world :** travelling through the world □ **kept my eyes
open :** been on the look-out □ **prevalent :** common, wide-spread
one : profession
acknowledge : recognize □ **reticence :** silence, discretion
not till : only when □ **become closely acquainted with them :** got to
know them better, more intimately □ **played cards :** N.B. the zero
article before games (≠ **music :** play *the* piano, violin, etc.)
living : cf. standard, cost of living □ **disinclination :** reluctance,
unwillingness □ **enlarge upon :** explain more fully □ **craft :** trade,
profession □ **passing themselves off for :** pretending to be
landed proprietors : landowners □ **snobbish :** *snobbery* makes *snobs*
for the novelist to study : for the novelist who wishes to study them
my good fortune : my (good) luck; I have been lucky
affable : friendly; pleasant, likeable □ **obliging :** helpful
hinted : suggested, implied; given a hint □ **however discreetly :** no
matter how diplomatically, even when using the utmost discretion
calling : vocation, profession □ **no sooner... than :** hardly, scarcely...
when □ **shy :** reticent, withdrawn □ **airy :** nonchalant □ **on my part :**
from me □ **stacking the cards :** (*fam* & *Am*) cheating at cards □
assume the appearance : look like □ **clam** = *praire*
hope for : expect
the oblique (method)
childlike : innocent, artless, like a child □ **bland :** diplomatic to the
point of being enigmatic □ **sympathy :** 1) compassion 2) liking
confessed : admitted □ **a word ∅ I had written :** N.B. zero relative

obscurely : dimly, instinctively
Philistine : uncultured; lowbrow □ **indulgence :** (without) tolerance
gather : assemble, collect □ **bold :** audacious □ **surmise** *(lit)* guess,
supposition □ **industry :** hard work

It may be imagined with what enthusiasm I made the acquaintance a little while ago of two gentlemen who seemed likely to add appreciably to my small store of information. I was travelling from Haiphong on a French liner going East, and they joined the ship at Hong-Kong. They had gone there for the races and were now on their way back to Shanghai. I was going there too, and thence to Peking. I soon learned that they had come from New York for a trip, were bound for Peking also, and by a happy 10 coincidence meant to return to America in the ship in which I had myself booked a passage. I was naturally attracted to them, for they were pleasant fellows, but it was not till a fellow-passenger warned me that they were professional gamblers that I settled down to complete enjoyment of their acquaintance. I had no hope that they would ever discuss with frankness their interesting occupation, but I expected from a hint here, from a casual remark there, to learn some very useful things.

One —Campbell was his name— was a man in the late 20 thirties, small, but so well built as not to look short, slender, with large, melancholy eyes and beautiful hands. But for a premature baldness he would have been more than commonly good-looking. He was neatly dressed. He spoke slowly, in a low voice, and his movements were deliberate. The other was made on another pattern. He was a big, burly man with a red face and crisp black hair, of powerful appearance, strong in the arm and pugnacious. His name was Peterson.

The merits of the combination were obvious. The elegant, 30 exquisite Campbell had the subtle brain, the knowledge of character, and the deft hands; but the hazards of the card-

it may be imagined : anyone may imagine □ **with what enthusiasm** : how enthusiastically □ **a little while ago** : a short time ago
seemed likely to add : would probably add; seemed the kind of people who might add
liner : big boat sailing on a regular line □ **joined** : came on board; cf. join a political party □ **races** : horse-racing □ **on their way back** : on their return journey □ **thence** *(lit)* : from there
learned : found out
trip : excursion □ **bound for** : on their way to
meant : intended
booked : reserved □ **passage** : trip; berth
pleasant : nice; affable, likeable □ **fellows** *(fam)* : chaps; men □ **not till** : only when □ **fellow-passenger** : another passenger □ **warned** : put me on my guard □ **gamblers** : who played for money □ **settled down** : made myself comfortable □ **to complete enjoyment of their acquaintance** : to enjoy their companionship completely □ **frankness** : openness; candour □ **hint** : suggestion □ **casual remark** : something said in passing
in the/his late thirties : between the ages of 36-39 ≠ *early* 30's
well built : well-proportioned □ **as not to look** : that he did not look □ **short** ≠ tall □ **slender** : slim ≠ fat □ **but for** : except for; had it not been for □ **premature baldness** : the fact that he had lost his hair early in life □ **more than commonly** : exceptionally □ **neatly** : elegantly □ **low** : soft ≠ loud
on another pattern : on a different model □ **burly** : muscular and heavily built □ **crisp** : strong and very curly
pugnacious : combative; a fighter

obvious : evident, clear □ **subtle** : ingenious, shrewd; full of subtlety
brain : mind, intelligence
deft : clever, skilful □ **hazards** : dangers due to chance

sharper's life are many, and when it came to a scrap Peterson's ready fist must often have proved invaluable. I do not know how it spread through the ship so quickly that a blow of Peterson's would stretch any man out. But during the short voyage from Hong-Kong to Shanghai they never even suggested a game of cards. Perhaps they had done well during the race-week and felt entitled to a holiday. They were certainly enjoying the advantages of not living for the time in a dry country and I do not think I do them an injustice if I say that for the most part they were far from sober. Each one talked little of himself but willingly of the other. Campbell informed me that Peterson was one of the most distinguished mining engineers in New York and Peterson assured me that Campbell was an eminent banker. He said that his wealth was fabulous. And who was I not to accept ingenuously all that was told me? But I thought it negligent of Campbell not to wear jewellery of a more expensive character. It seemed to me that to use a silver cigarette-case was rather careless.

I stayed but a day in Shanghai, and though I met the pair again in Peking I was then so much engaged that I saw little of them. I thought it a little odd that Campbell should spend his entire time in the hotel. I do not think he even went to see the Temple of Heaven. But I could quite understand that from his point of view Peking was unsatisfactory and I was not surprised when the pair returned to Shanghai, where, I knew the wealthy merchants played for big money. I met them again in the ship that was to take us across the Pacific and I could not but sympathize with my friends when I saw that the passengers were little inclined to gamble. There were no rich people among them. It was a dull crowd.

sharper : professional cheat □ **scrap** *(fam)* : fight
ready : alert □ **fist** = *poing* □ **proved** : shown themselves, turned out
□ **invaluable** : precious □ **spread through** : (the rumour) went all
over □ **a blow of Peterson's** : a punch from Peterson □ **stretch...
out** : knock (any man) out □ **voyage** : sea trip, sea journey
suggested : hinted at
race-week : week of horse-racing □ **entitled** : they had a right (to)
enjoying : benefitting from □ **for the time** : temporarily; for the time
being □ **dry** : that restricted the sale of alcoholic drinks □ **I do them
an injustice** : I am unjust, unfair to them □ **for the most part** : mostly
sober ≠ drunk □ **willingly** : unreluctantly readily

eminent : prominent
his wealth was fabulous : he was fabulously rich, wealthy
ingenuously : innocently, naïvely □ **I thought it negligent of
Campbell** : I considered it (was) careless on the part of Campbell
expensive : valuable □ **silver** = *argent*
cigarette-case : for keeping cigarettes □ **rather careless** : a little
negligent □ **I stayed but a day** *(lit)* : I only spent a day □ **though**
I met : in spite of meeting □ **I saw little of them** *(idiom)* : I didn't
see them very much; cf. I didn't see much of them □ **odd** : strange
his entire time : the whole of his time; all his time
I could quite understand : it was quite understandable to me
from his point of view : to his eyes, to his mind
the pair : the two of them
wealthy : rich, affluent □ **played for big money** : gambled for high
stakes □ **was to** : was supposed to, was scheduled
I could not but sympathize with : I could not help being sorry for
were little inclined : were rather reluctant, disinclined
dull : boring ≠ interesting, exciting

Campbell indeed suggested a game of poker, but no one would play more than twenty-dollar table stakes, and Peterson, evidently not thinking it worth while, would not join. Although we played afternoon and evening through the journey he sat down with us only on the last day. I suppose he thought he might just as well make his bar chits, and this he did very satisfactorily in a single sitting. But Campbell evidently loved the game for itself. Of course it is only if you have a passion for the business by which you
10 earn your living that you can make a success of it. The stakes were nothing to him and he played all day and every day. It fascinated me to see the way in which he dealt the cards, very slowly, with his delicate hands. His eyes seemed to bore through the back of each one. He drank heavily, but remained quiet and self-controlled. His face was expressionless. I judged him to be a perfect card-player and I wished that I could see him at work. It increased my esteem for him to see that he could take what was only a relaxation so seriously.

20   I parted with the pair at Victoria and concluded that I should never see them again. I set about sorting my impressions and made notes of the various points that I thought would prove useful.

When I arrived in New York I found an invitation to luncheon at the Ritz with an old friend of mine. When I went she said to me:

"It's quite a small party. A man is coming whom I think you'll like. He's a prominent banker; he's bringing a friend with him."

30   The words were hardly out of her mouth when I saw coming up to us Campbell and Peterson. The truth flashed

34

indeed : certainly; admittedly □ **suggested :** proposed
table stakes = *enjeux*
not thinking it worth while : considering it not worth playing
join : participate; cf. join a club □ **afternoon and evening :** every
afternoon and evening □ **through the journey :** during the whole trip
make his bar chits : win enough money to pay his chits (i.e. bills)
for drinks at the bar □ **a single sitting :** in only one session
for itself : for its own sake

make a success of it : be successful at it: succeed in it
were nothing to him : meant nothing to him, did not matter to him
the way in which : how □ **dealt :** handed out, distributed

bore through : pierce, see through □ **drank heavily :** drank a lot; was
a heavy drinker (cf. a heavy smoker) □ **expressionless :** blank
I wished I could see him at work : I regretted not being able to see
him at work □ **increased :** raised, augmented □ **esteem :** respect
take... seriously : treat seriously

I parted with : left; separated from □ **the pair :** the two of them
set about : began, started □ **sorting :** arranging; putting in order

prove useful : show themselves to be useful; turn out to be useful

an old friend of mine : one of my old friends
went : i.e. arrived at the luncheon
quite a small party : not a very big party
prominent : eminent, famous
the words... mouth when... : hardly had she spoken *when*; no sooner
had she spoken *than* □ **the truth :** reality □ **flashed across me :**

across me: Campbell really was an opulent banker; Peterson really was a distinguished engineer; they were not card-sharpers at all. I flatter myself I kept my face, but as I blandly shook hands with them I muttered under my breath furiously:

"Impostors!"

came to me in a flash, as quickly as a flash of lightning
distinguished: well-known, eminent, prominent
card-sharpers: cheats □ **I kept my face**: I showed no emotion
blandly: expressionlessly, enigmatically □ **muttered**: grumbled
under my breath: to myself ≠ aloud, out loud

Grammaire au fil des nouvelles

Traduisez les phrases suivantes inspirées du texte (le premier chiffre renvoie à la page, les suivants aux lignes).

Leur réticence est telle que ce n'est qu'après avoir fait vraiment connaissance avec eux qu'on découvre comment ils gagnent leur vie (not till... closely acquainted ...earn their... life? ... their *living*? 28 - 6).

Ils se font passer volontiers pour des officiers de cavalerie (we all have out weaknesses... 28 - 12).

Il était si bien proportionné qu'il ne paraissait pas petit (he had a good figure, a good build, 30 - 20).

Si ce n'avait été une calvitie précoce, il aurait été plus beau que la moyenne (*if it hadn't been for,* en 2 mots, 30 - 21).

La plupart du temps ils étaient loin d'être à jeun (*most of the time,* ou bien *for the most +?... drunk ≠?* 32 - 10).

Je ne restais qu'un jour à Shanghai (*syn.* de *only = 32 - 20).

Il me semblait un peu bizarre que Campbell passât tout son temps à l'hôtel (après un jugement un subjonctif en français — et en anglais comment fait-on ? 32 - 22).

Je les rencontrai à nouveau sur le bateau à bord duquel nous devions faire la traversée du Pacifique (it was going to take us across the Pacific — according to plan! 32 - 28).

Nous jouions tous les après-midi et tous les soirs pendant toute la traversée (*tous les =* impliqué plutôt qu'exprimé, 34 - 4).

Ce n'est que lorsque vous êtes passionné par ce qui vous permet de gagner votre vie que vous y réussissez (his life was a success; he was a success; he made a success... 34 - 8,9,10).

J'étais fasciné par la manière dont il distribuait les cartes (commençons par : *it fascinated me to see...* 34 - 12).

Je souhaitais avoir l'occasion de le voir au travail (*I wished to be able* est un peu péremptoire : *I wished I...* 34 - 16).

Il prenait au sérieux ce qui n'était qu'une détente pour lui (we relax; we enjoy cards as a serious rel...? 34 - 18).

J'étais invité à déjeuner par une vieille amie à moi (an old friend of whose? 34 - 25).

À peine avais-je prononcé ces mots que je vis Campbell qui venait à notre rencontre (hardly...when; no sooner...than, 34 - 30).

The Ant
and the Grasshopper

   Generations of schoolboys have no doubt been impressed — and possibly depressed — by the moralizing of La
Fontaine whose fables enjoy international fame. Somerset
Maugham seems to have said to himself that if these fables
are worthy of their reputation, they must represent eternal
truths. They must still be valid for people living in this
modern world of ours. Let's look around, observe people's
lives and careers, and see whether virtue is rewarded and
vice punished as regularly as La Fontaine would lead us to
suppose...

When I was a very small boy I was made to learn by heart certain of the fables of La Fontaine, and the moral of each was carefully explained to me. Among those I learnt was *The Ant and the Grasshopper*, which is devised to bring home to the young the useful lesson that in an imperfect world industry is rewarded and giddiness punished. In this admirable fable (I apologize for telling something which everyone is politely, but inexactly, supposed to know) the ant spends a laborious summer gathering its winter store,

10 while the grasshopper sits on a blade of grass singing to the sun. Winter comes and the ant is comfortably provided for, but the grasshopper has an empty larder: he goes to the ant and begs for a little food. Then the ant gives him her classic answer:

"What were you doing in the summer time?"

"Saving your presence, I sang, I sang all day, all night."

"You sang. Why, then go and dance."

I do not ascribe it to perversity on my part, but rather to the inconsequence of childhood, which is deficient in moral

20 sense, that I could never quite reconcile myself to the lesson. My sympathies were with the grasshopper and for some time I never saw an ant without putting my foot on it. In this summary (and as I have discovered since, entirely human) fashion I sought to express my disapproval of prudence and common sense.

I could not help thinking of this fable when the other day I saw George Ramsay lunching by himself in a restaurant. I never saw anyone wear an expression of such deep gloom. He was staring into space. He looked as though the burden

30 of the whole world sat on his shoulders. I was sorry for him: I suspected at once that his unfortunate brother had been

I was made to learn: someone made me learn (N.B. *to* before the infinitive in the passive form) □ **moral**: lesson (N.B. *morale* = state of mind = *le moral*) □ **explained**: elucidated

ant = *fourmi* □ **grasshopper** = *cigale* □ **devised**: conceived □ **bring home**: teach, make (young people) realise

industry: hard work □ **rewarded**: recompensed □ **giddiness** *(lit)* ≠ industry □ **punished** ≠ rewarded □ **apologize**: ask to be excused, forgiven □ **everyone is supposed to know**: people suppose that everybody knows □ **laborious**: hard-working □ **gathering**: collecting □ **winter store**: provisions for the cold season □ **blade**: leaf, stem □ **provided for**: supplied (with food)

larder: where food is stored in a house

begs for food: asks humbly for something to eat

were you doing: N.B. durative aspect of the verb

saving your presence: *(lit)* sorry! I apologize

why: in that case □ **go and dance** (note *and* after *go* and *come*)

ascribe: attribute □ **on my part**: as far as I am concerned

inconsequence: unthinking nature □ **deficient**: lackiing

reconcile myself to: bring (persuade) myself to agree with

my sympathies were with: I was on the side of

putting my foot on it: stamping treading on it □ **in this summary...**

fashion: in this brief, perfunctory manner

sought *(seek, sought, sought)*: tried attempted

common sense: being sensible, reasonable

help thinking: avoid thinking, prevent myself from thinking

lunching: having his mid-day meal □ **by himself**: all alone

wear *(wore, worn)*: have (clothes, hair, smile, scowl, etc.) □ **gloom**: melancholy □ **staring**: gazing □ **burden**: weight, problems

sat: were placed □ **shoulders** = *épaules* □ **was sorry for him**: pitied him □ **unfortunate**: here = unlucky for the others

41

causing trouble again. I went up to him and held out my hand.

"How are you?" I asked.

"I'm not in hilarious spirits," he answered.

"Is it Tom again?"

He sighed.

"Yes, it's Tom again."

"Why don't you chuck him? You've done everything in the world for him. You must know by now that he's quite
10 hopeless."

I suppose every family has a black sheep. Tom had been a sore trial to his for twenty years. He had begun life decently enough: he went into business, married, and had two children. The Ramsays were perfectly respectable people and there was every reason to suppose that Tom Ramsay would have a useful and honourable career. But one day, without warning, he announced that he didn't like work and that he wasn't suited for marriage. He wanted to enjoy himself. He would listen to no expostulations. He left
20 his wife and his office. He had a little money and he spent two happy years in the various capitals of Europe. Rumours of his doings reached his relations from time to time and they were profoundly shocked. He certainly had a very good time. They shook their heads and asked what would happen when his money was spent. They soon found out: he borrowed. He was charming and unscrupulous. I have never met anyone to whom it was more difficult to refuse a loan. He made a steady income from his friends and he made friends easily. But he always said that the money you
30 spent on necessities was boring; the money that was amusing to spend was the money you spent on luxuries. For this he depended on his brother George. He did not waste

42

causing trouble: the source of difficulty and worry □ **held** *(hold, held, held)*: reached, stretched (in order to shake hands with him)
how are you?: is your health (business) good?
in hilarious spirit: in a merry (joyful) mood (frame of mind)

sighed: breathed out heavily to show his sadness; heaved a sigh

chuck: drop, leave (him) to fend for himself
by now = emphatic form of *now* □ **quite**: absolutely, completely
hopeless: irrecuperable; a hopeless case
black sheep: disreputable member
sore: here = great trial ordeal, source of trouble; very trying
decently: respectably □ **went into business**: took up a commercial career; business is business □ **married**: got married (to someone)
every reason to suppose = every reason for supposing
useful ≠ useless
without warning: unexpectedly; to everyone's surprise
wasn't suited for marriage: didn't suit marriage
enjoy himself: enjoy life □ **expostulations**: remonstrances
wife: the woman he had married, was married to
capitals: capital cities □ **rumours**: stories, unconfirmed news
doings: activities □ **relations**: members of the family
had a very good time: enjoyed himself (life) a great deal
shook: moved (their heads) from side to side disapprovingly
happen: take place □ **spent**: finished □ **found out**: discovered
borrowed: asked others for money (a loan of money) □
unscrupulous: without scruples (note the spelling)
steady income: regular revenue, living
made friends: made friends with people, struck up friendships
boring ≠ exciting; a bore; a source of boredom
luxuries: luxurious things; luxury goods
depended on: counted (relied) on □ **waste**: use needlessly

43

his charm on him. George was a serious man and insensible to such enticements. George was respectable. Once or twice he fell to Tom's promises of amendment and gave him considerable sums in order that he might make a fresh start. On these Tom bought a motor-car and some very nice jewellery. But when circumstances forced George to realize that his brother would never settle down and he washed his hands of him, Tom, without a qualm, began to blackmail him. It was not very nice for a respectable lawyer to find his 10 brother shaking cocktails behind the bar of his favourite restaurant or to see him waiting on the box-seat of a taxi outside his club. Tom said that to serve in a bar or to drive a taxi was a perfectly decent occupation, but if George could oblige him with a couple of hundred pounds he didn't mind for the honour of the family giving it up. George paid.

Once Tom nearly went to prison. George was terribly upset. He went into the whole discreditable affair. Really Tom had gone too far. He had been wild, thoughtless, and 20 selfish, but he had never before done anything dishonest, by which George meant illegal; and if he were prosecuted he would assuredly be convicted. But you cannot allow your only brother to go to gaol. The man Tom had cheated, a man called Cronshaw, was vindictive. He was determined to take the matter into court; he said Tom was a scoundrel and should be punished. It cost George an infinite deal of trouble and five hundred pounds to settle the affair. I have never seen him in such a rage as when he heard that Tom and Cronshaw had gone off together to Monte Carlo the 30 moment they cashed the cheque. They spent a happy month there.

on: note the preposition: spend, waste time (money) *on*...
enticements: temptations, incitements, incentives
fell to: was duped, taken in by □ **amendment**: improved behaviour
in order... start: (in order) for him to turn over a new leaf
on these: i.e. on those (sums of money)
jewellery *(uncountable noun)* = jewels
settle down: become respectable, stop sowing his wild oats
qualm: scruple □ **blackmail**: extort money by menaces
nice: pleasant □ **lawyer**: someone in the legal profession
shaking *(shook, shaken)*: mixing in a shaker
box-seat: driver's seat
drive *(drove, driven)* **a taxi**: be a taxi-driver, a cabby
decent: respectable
oblige him with: give, let him have □ **couple**: two, three or more
mind... giving it up: object to abandoning, renouncing it
paid *(pay, paid, paid)*: gave him the sum of money
nearly went to prison: just escaped going to prison
upset: sad, distressed □ **went into**: investigated □ **discreditable**:
scandalous □ **wild**: undisciplined □ **thoughtless**: careless, reckless
selfish: egoistic, egotistic □ **dishonest** ≠ honest
prosecuted: taken to court, sued
convicted: found guilty; sentenced to prison or a fine □ **your only**
brother: your one brother; an only child □ **gaol**: prison □ **cheated**:
deceived, swindled □ **was determined**: had decided
take the matter into court: prosecute, sue □ **scoundrel**: criminal,
swindler □ **it cost George** *(cost, cost, cost)*: it took George □ **an**
infinite deal of trouble: infinitely great efforts □ **settle the affair**:
find a solution for the affair, solve the affair

the moment they cashed the cheque: as soon as they got the money
for the cheque

For twenty years Tom raced and gambled, philandered with the prettiest girls, danced, ate in the most expensive restaurants, and dressed beautifully. He always looked as if he had just stepped out of a bandbox. Though he was forty-six you would never have taken him for more than thirty-five. He was a most amusing companion and though you knew he was perfectly worthless you could not but enjoy his society. He had high spirits, an unfailing gaiety, and incredible charm. I never grudged the contributions he
10 regularly levied on me for the necessities of his existence. I never lent him fifty pounds without feeling that I was in his debt. Tom Ramsay knew everyone and everyone knew Tom Ramsay. You could not approve of him, but you could not help liking him.

Poor George, only a year older than his scapegrace brother, looked sixty. He had never taken more than a fortnight's holiday in the year for a quarter of a century. He was in his office every morning at nine-thirty and never left it till six. He was honest, industrious, and worthy. He had
20 a good wife, to whom he had never been unfaithful even in thought, and four daughters to whom he was the best of fathers. He made a point of saving a third of his income and his plan was to retire at fifty-five to a little house in the country where he proposed to cultivate his garden and play golf. His life was blameless. He was glad that he was growing old because Tom was growing old too. He rubbed his hands and said :

"It was all very well when Tom was young and good-looking, but he's only a year younger than I am. In four
30 years he'll be fifty. He won't find life so easy then. I shall have thirty thousand pounds by the time I'm fifty. For

46

raced: attended horse races □ **gambled**: played cards etc. for money □ **philandered**: flirted (with), made love (to) □ **ate** *(eat, ate, eaten)*: had meals □ **expensive**: costly □ **dressed beautifully**: wore the most beautiful clothes □ **stepped**: emerged □ **bandbox**: box given by a tailor □ **forty-six**: 46 years old (of age) □ **taken him for**: thought he was □ **amusing companion**: entertaining friend

worthless: a good-for-nothing □ **could not but enjoy**: could not help enjoying □ **had high spirits**: was full of fun □ **unfailing**: invariable; his gaiety never failed him □ **grudged**: regretted; gave unwillingly □ **levied on me**: extracted from me, as if he were levying a tax □ **lent** *(lend, lent, lent)* ≠ borrow □ **in his debt**: indebted to him □ **knew** *(know, knew, known)*: was acquainted, was friends with

approve of him: give your approval of him □ **could not help liking him**: could not but like him

his scapegrace brother: his good-for-nothing of a brother

a fortnight's holiday: note the genitive to quantify duration
nine-thirty: note the official way of saying "half past nine"
industrious: full of industry; hard-working □ **worthy**: virtuous
to whom... unfaithful: whom he had never deceived, betrayed
in thought ≠ by act, in reality, in actual fact
point: principle □ **saving**: economizing □ **his income**: the money he earned □ **retire**: go into retirement
proposed: intended □ **cultivate his garden**: do gardening
blameless: irreproachable; you couldn't blame him for anything
growing *(grow, grew, grown)*: becoming □ **rubbed his hands**: made a motion with his hands to show his satisfaction
it was all very well: it was plain sailing; there were no problems □ **good-looking**: handsome, elegant □ **in four years**: within (another) four years □ **by the time I'm fifty**: when I'm fifty (years old)
for... years: N.B. *for* to introduce duration

twenty-five years I've said that Tom would end in the gutter. And we shall see how he likes that. We shall see if it really pays best to work or be idle."

Poor George! I sympathized with him. I wondered now as I sat down beside him what infamous thing Tom had done. George was evidently very much upset.

"Do you know what's happened now?" he asked me.

I was prepared for the worst. I wondered if Tom had got into the hands of the police at last. George could hardly
10 bring himself to speak.

"You're not going to deny that all my life I've been hardworking, decent, respectable, and straightforward. After a life of industry and thrift I can look forward to retiring on a small income in gilt-edged securities. I've always done my duty in that state of life in which it has pleased Providence to place me."

"True."

"And you can't deny that Tom has been an idle, worthless dissolute, and dishonourable rogue. If there were any justice
20 he'd be in the workhouse."

"True."

George grew red in the face.

"A few weeks ago he became engaged to a woman old enough to be his mother. And now she's died and left him everything she had. Half a million pounds, a yacht, a house in London, and a house in the country."

George Ramsay beat his clenched fist on the table.

"It's not fair, I tell you, it's not fair. Damn it, it's not fair."

30   I could not help it. I burst into a shout of laughter as I looked at George's wrathful face, I rolled in my chair, I very

48

gutter: street, i.e. poverty

how he likes that: how much he likes that; whether he likes that □

see if it pays best: see whether it is most profitable □ **idle**: lazy

I sympathized with him: I was sorry for him □ **wondered**: asked myself □ **infamous**: horrible, dreadful, appalling

evidently: obviously □ **upset**: distressed, disturbed, disconcerted

happened: occurred, taken place

worst ≠ best □ **got into the hands of**: got into trouble with; been caught by □ **George could hardly bring himself to speak**: it was difficult (hard) for George to find the courage to speak

deny ≠ confirm

hardworking: industrious □ **decent**: honourable □ **straightforward**: honest □ **industry**: hard work □ **thrift**: economizing □ **look forward to retiring**: hope to retire □ **gilt-edged securities** = *placements de père de famille* □ **done my duty**: been dutiful □ **state of life**: status

true: (that's) true; I agree; I don't deny it

idle: lazy, ≠ hardworking □ **worthless**: immoral, unprincipled

dissolute: debauched □ **rogue**: scoundrel; unscrupulous person

workhouse: institution for destitute people, paupers

grew red in the face: flushed; turned red, crimson

engaged to: affianced to (note the preposition) □ **woman old enough**: woman (who was) old enough

everything she had: everything (that) she had

beat *(beat, beat, beaten)*: hit, pounded □ **clenched fist** = *poing*

fair: just, right □ **damn it** *(excl)*: hell, blast

help: prevent, avoid □ **burst into a shout of laughter**: burst out laughing □ **wrathful**: angry, furious

nearly fell on the floor. George never forgave me. But Tom often asks me to excellent dinners in his charming house in Mayfair, and if he occasionally borrows a trifle from me, that is merely from force of habit. It is never more than a sovereign.

asks me to... dinners: invites me to... dinners
Mayfair: fashionable district in London □ **borrows** ≠ lends □ **a trifle:** here = a small sum of money □ **merely:** simply, only
sovereign: gold coin worth one pound sterling

Grammaire au fil des nouvelles

Traduisez les phrases suivantes inspirées du texte (le premier chiffre renvoie à la page, les suivants aux lignes).

Quand j'étais un tout petit garçon, on me faisait apprendre par cœur certaines fables de La Fontaine (structure causative : *they made me learn...* mais mettons tout cela au passif, 40 - 1).

La fourmi passe l'été à ramasser laborieusement un stock de nourriture pour l'hiver (*spend* + infinitif ou *-ing*? 40 -9).

L'hiver venu, la fourmi se trouve confortablement pourvue (*the winter store provides for the ant's comfort...* et au passif : *the ant is comfortably...* 40 - 11).

Je ne pouvais m'empêcher de penser à cette fable (*prevent from thinking*, mais plus idiomatique = ? 40 - 26).

Il avait l'air de quelqu'un qui porterait sur ses épaules tout le malheur du monde (malheur = *burden...* le conditionnel de la proposition relative se traduit comment ? 40 - 29).

Il entra dans les affaires (droit, 42 - 13).

Il dépendait de son frère George (depend, rely + ? 42 - 32).

Il lui donna des sommes considérables pour qu'il puisse repartir du pied droit (for him to be able ou in order/so that...fresh start, 44 - 4).

Il ne voyait pas d'objection à y renoncer (...mind? 44 - 15).

Vous ne pouvez pas tolérer que votre seul frère aille en prison (can you allow it? 44 - 22,23).

Dès qu'ils touchèrent le chèque ils partirent pour Monte Carlo (*as soon as* ou *the moment...* 44 - 29,30).

On ne pouvait que s'amuser en sa compagnie (on = *we? you? they?* évitons en tout cas one (*lit*) 46 - 7,8).

Il mettait un point d'honneur à économiser un tiers de son revenu (*a point* sera toujours honorable en anglais, 46 - 22).

Il était content de vieillir parce que Tom était en train de vieillir aussi (forme simple ou progressive ? 46 - 25,26).

Je m'attendais au pire (commençons : *I was prepared...* 48 - 8).

Il y a quelques semaines il s'est fiancé (*tps du v?* 48 - 23).

The Happy Man

A first unexpected meeting in London between two
perfect strangers. It is not until many years later that the
same two people meet again, by pure chance, in Seville.

Yet one of the men, a doctor, not only gives the other a
free medical consultation, but also insists that it is he, the
doctor, who is in the other's debt. What is it that forms a
link between these two men?

It is a dangerous thing to order the lives of others and I have often wondered at the self-confidence of politicians, reformers and suchlike who are prepared to force upon their fellows measures that must alter their manners, habits, and points of view. I have always hesitated to give advice, for how can one advise another how to act unless one knows that other as well as one knows oneself? Heaven knows, I know little enough of myself: I know nothing of others. We can only guess at the thoughts and emotions of our
10 neighbours. Each one of us is a prisoner in a solitary tower and he communicates with the other prisoners, who form mankind, by conventional signs that have not quite the same meaning for them as for himself. And life, unfortunately, is something that you can lead but once; mistakes are often irreparable, and who am I that I should tell this one and that how he should lead it? Life is a difficult business and I have found it hard enough to make my own a complete and rounded thing; I have not been tempted to teach my neighbour what he should do with his. But there
20 are men who flounder at the journey's start, the way before them is confused and hazardous, and on occasion, however unwillingly, I have been forced to point the finger of fate. Sometimes men have said to me, what shall I do with my life? and I have seen myself for a moment wrapped in the dark cloak of Destiny.

Once I know that I advised well.

I was a young man and I lived in a modest apartment in London near Victoria Station. Late one afternoon, when I was beginning to think that I had worked enough for that
30 day, I heard a ring at the bell. I opened the door to a total stranger. He asked me my name; I told him. He asked if he might come in.

order : organize, regulate
wondered : marvelled, been amazed □ **self-confidence** : assurance □
politicians : men in politics □ **suchlike** : people like that
fellows : other people □ **alter** : change (for better or worse)
points of view : opinions, viewpoints □ **advice** *(U)* : counsel(s)
unless one knows : if one does not know
Heaven knows *(excl)* : God knows

guess at : make conjectures about
neighbours : people we meet or who live near us □ **tower** = *tour*

mankind : the community of men, of human beings
meaning : sense, significance
unfortunately : unhappily, unluckily □ **lead** : here = have, live □ **but
once** : only once □ **who... tell** : what competence have I to tell
this one and that : this man or that (man); any person
hard : difficult □ **make my own** : transform my own (life) into
rounded : well integrated
teach *(taught, taught)* : give lessons
flounder : are lost, in a muddle □ **journey's start** : the beginning of
their itinerary (through life) □ **hazardous** : full of unpredictable
dangers □ **however unwillingly** : even if I am very unwilling □ **point
the finger of fate** : show the path which will be their fate destiny
wrapped : enveloped, dressed
cloak : cape
once : one time only

late one afternoon : one late (≠ early) afternoon

I heard a ring : I heard someone ring (ing) □ **bell** = *sonnette*
stranger : someone I did not know; he was a stranger to me □ **if
he might** : if he could, whether I would allow him to

"Certainly."

I led him into my sitting-room and begged him to sit down. He seemed a trifle embarrassed. I offered him a cigarette and he had some difficulty in lighting it without letting go of his hat. When he had satisfactorily achieved this feat I asked him if I should not put it on a chair for him. He quickly did this and while doing it dropped his umbrella.

"I hope you don't mind my coming to see you like this," he said. "My name is Stephens and I am a doctor. You're in the medical, I believe?"

"Yes, but I don't practise."

"No, I know. I've just read a book of yours about Spain and I wanted to ask you about it."

"It's not a very good book, I'm afraid."

"The fact remains that you know something about Spain and there's no one else I know who does. And I thought perhaps you wouldn't mind giving me some information."

"I shall be very glad."

He was silent for a moment. He reached out for his hat and holding it in one hand absent-mindedly stroked it with the other. I surmised that it gave him confidence.

"I hope you won't think it very odd for a perfect stranger to talk to you like this." He gave an apologetic laugh. "I'm not going to tell you the story of my life."

When people say this to me I always know that it is precisely what they are going to do. I do not mind. In fact I rather like it.

"I was brought up by two old aunts. I've never been anywhere. I've never done anything. I've been married for

56

certainly : of course

led *(lead, led, led)* : showed □ **begged** : asked, requested

a trifle : a little, somewhat

difficulty in lighting it : trouble in Ø lighting it

letting go of his hat : letting his hat go □ **achieved** : succeeded in

feat : difficult task □ **should not** : : had better not

dropped his umbrella : let his umbrella fall

mind my coming : object to my/me coming; object if I come

in the medical : i.e. in the medical (profession), in medicine

practise : exercise my profession; I'm not in practice

a book of yours : one of your books

ask you about it : i.e. ask you (a question) about it

I'm afraid : here = I'm sorry (to say) i.e. an apologetic tone

the fact remains : it is still true

no one else : no other person

some information : note this uncountable noun

glad : pleased; it will be a pleasure

for a moment : note *for* to introduce duration □ **reached** : stretched

absent-mindedly : unconsciously □ **stroked** : caressed

surmised : supposed, assumed, guessed □ **confidence** : assurance

odd for... talk : bizarre that a perfect stranger should talk

apologetic : as an apology, an excuse

say this to me : tell me this

I do not mind : I do not care, I do not object

I rather like it : I quite like it

brought up : reared, raised □ **been anywhere here** : travelled to any
other place; have you been *to* England? Note the preposition

six years. I have no children. I'm a medical officer at the Camberwell Infirmary. I can't stick it any more."

There was something very striking in the short, sharp sentences he used. They had a forcible ring. I had not given him more than a cursory glance, but now I looked at him with curiosity. He was a little man, thick-set and stout, of thirty perhaps, with a round red face from which shone small, dark and very bright eyes. His black hair was cropped close to a bullet-shaped head. He was dressed in a blue suit a good deal the worse for wear. It was baggy at the knees and the pockets bulged untidily.

"You know what the duties are of a medical officer in an infirmary. One day is pretty much like another. And that's all I've got to look forward to for the rest of my life. Do you think it's worth it?"

"It's a means of livelihood," I answered.

"Yes, I know. The money's pretty good."

"I don't exactly know why you've come to me."

"Well, I wanted to know whether you thought there would be any chance for an English doctor in Spain?"

"Why Spain?"

"I don't know, I just have a fancy for it."

"It's not like *Carmen*, you know."

"But there's sunshine there, and there's good wine, and there's colour, and there's air you can breathe. Let me say what I have to say straight out. I heard by accident that there was no English doctor in Seville. Do you think I could earn a living there? Is it madness to give up a good safe job for an uncertainty?"

"What does your wife think about it?"

"She's willing."

"It's a great risk."

58

medical officer : doctor

infirmary : hospital (often a large one) □ **stick** : *(fam)* bear, stand

striking : surprising □ **short** ≠ long □ **sharp** : abrupt, staccato, brusque □ **forcible** : strong, compelling □ **ring** : sound; they rang true

cursory : passing, casual □ **glance** : quick look

thick-set : short and broad □ **stout** : corpulent

shone *(shine, shone, shone)* : radiated

dark ≠ light □ **bright** : shining, brilliant □ **cropped** : cut short, clipped □ **bullet-shaped** : having the shape of a bullet you fire from a gun □ **the worse for wear** : it had suffered from being worn □ **baggy** : out of shap □ **knees** = *genoux* □ **bulged** : were distended □ **untidily** : inelegantly □ **duties** : work

pretty like another : more or less like another

to look forward to : to hope for, in store for me

worth it : worth doing; is this life worth living?

a means of livelihood : a way of earning one's living

pretty good : quite good, rather good, very good

to know whether : to find out if

chance : opportunity, opening

why Spain? : why choose Spain? Why have you chosen Spain?

have a fancy : have an inclination, a preference, a liking

there's sunshine : the sun shines there

air you can breathe : air worth breathing

straight out : directly, without beating about the bush

earn a living : make a livelihood □ **give up** : abandon □ **safe** : secure □ **job** : position, post, career

what does your wife think about it? : what's your wife's opinion?

willing : ready (to try); in agreement

great risk : very risky

"I know. But if you say take it, I will: if you say stay where you are, I'll stay."

He was looking at me intently with those bright dark eyes of his and I knew that he meant what he said. I reflected for a moment.

"Your whole future is concerned: you must decide for yourself. But this I can tell you: if you don't want money but are content to earn just enough to keep body and soul together, then go. For you will lead a wonderful life."

10 He left me, I thought about him for a day or two, and then forgot. The episode passed completely from my memory.

Many years later, fifteen at least, I happened to be in Seville and having some trifling indisposition asked the hotel porter whether there was an English doctor in the town. He said there was and gave me the address. I took a cab and as I drove up to the house a little fat man came out of it. He hesitated when he caught sight of me.

"Have you come to see me?" he said. "I'm the English
20 doctor."

I explained my errand and he asked me to come in. He lived in an ordinary Spanish house, with a patio, and his consulting room which led out of it was littered with papers, books, medical appliances, and lumber. The sight of it would have startled a squeamish patient. We did our business and then I asked the doctor what his fee was. He shook his head and smiled.

"There's no fee."

"Why on earth not?"

30 "Don't you remember me? Why, I'm here because of something you said to me. You changed my whole life for me. I'm Stephens."

60

take it: i.e. take the risk, run the risk

intently: attentively, closely □ **those... eyes of his** emphatic form = those eyes (which were) his □ **he meant** *(mean, meant, meant)* **what he said**: he was serious when he said this

concerned: involved, at stake □ **you must decide**: you've got to decide □ **this I can tell you**: emphatic form = I can tell you this

content: satisfied □ **keep body and soul together**: to live without luxury, with the bare necessities

left *(leave, left, left)* **he**: went away

forgot *(forget, forgot, forgotten)*: stopped thinking about him

I happened to be: I was by chance

trifling: minor, unimportant □ **indisposition**: illness

hotel porter: person at the hotel door or reception desk

there was: there was (one)

cab: taxi □ **drove** *(drive, drove, driven)*: drew up at the house

caught sight of me: caught a glimpse of me

have you come to see me?: am I the one you have come to see?

my errand: why I had come □ **asked... in**: invited me (to come) in

ordinary ≠ extraordinary, out of the ordinary

consulting room: surgery □ **led out of it** ≠ gave (looked) into it □ **littered**: encumbered □ **appliances**: apparatus □ **lumber**: bric-a-brac □ **startled**: surprised and frightened □ **squeamish**: delicate

fee: emoluments (for doctors, lawyers, schools, universities)

shook his head: gave a negative answer with the head

there's no fee: there isn't any fee, anything to pay

why on earth not: *emphatic* = why not

why: here expresses incredulity = but

for me: designates the beneficiary; cf. open the door for me

I had not the least notion what he was talking about. He reminded me of our interview, he repeated to me what we had said, and gradually, out of the night, a dim recollection of the incident came back to me.

"I was wondering if I'd ever see you again," he said, "I was wondering if ever I'd have a chance of thanking you for all you've done for me."

"It's been a success then?"

I looked at him. He was very fat now and bald, but his eyes twinkled gaily and his fleshy, red face bore an expression of perfect good-humour. The clothes he wore, terribly shabby they were, had been made obviously by a Spanish tailor and his hat was the wide-brimmed sombrero of the Spaniard. He looked to me as though he knew a good bottle of wine when he saw it. He had a dissipated, though entirely sympathetic, appearance. You might have hesitated to let him remove your appendix, but you could not have imagined a more delightful creature to drink a glass of wine with.

"Surely you were married?" I said.

"Yes. My wife didn't like Spain, she went back to Camberwell, she was more at home there."

"Oh, I'm sorry for that."

His black eyes flashed a bacchanalian smile. He really had somewhat the look of a young Silenus.

"Life is full of compensations," he murmured.

The words were hardly out of his mouth when a Spanish woman, no longer in her first youth, but still boldly and voluptuously beautiful, appeared at the door. She spoke to him in Spanish, and I could not fail to perceive that she was the mistress of the house.

As he stood at the door to let me out he said to me:

the least notion: the slightest (foggiest) idea
reminded me of our interview: recalled our meeting
gradually: little by little □ **dim**: vague □ **recollection**: memory

was wondering: kept asking myself
chance: opportunity

fat ≠ thin, slim, slender □ **bald**: hairless
twinkled: shone, sparkled □ **fleshy**: fat □ **bore** *(bear, bore, borne)*:
wore □ **good-humour**: cheerfulness; good-humoured □ **clothes**:
suit □ **shabby**: worn, threadbare □ **obviously**: evidently, clearly
the wide-brimmed sombrero: the sombrero with a wide brim
as though: as if

sympathetic: here = *sympathique* □ **appearance**: (physical) look
remove: take out □ **appendix**: organ able to cause appendicitis
delightful: charming □ **creature**: person (good or bad) □ **to drink
a glass of wine with**: with whom to drink a glass of wine
surely: word used to sollicit an answer = weren't you married?

she was more at home there: life suited her better there
I'm sorry for that: that's a shame; what a pity!
flashed... a smile: smiled for a flash (i.e. a split second)
look: ambiguous 1) appearance 2) expression in the eyes
murmured: whispered, said under his breath
hardly... when: no sooner... than
in her first youth: very young □ **boldly**: audaciously, daringly

could not fail to perceive: could not help perceiving

stood: was standing □ **let me out**: let me (go) out

63

"You told me when last I saw you that if I came here I should earn just enough money to keep body and soul together, but that I should lead a wonderful life. Well, I want to tell you that you were right. Poor I have been and poor I shall always be, but by heaven I've enjoyed myself. I wouldn't exchange the life I've had with that of any king in the world."

when last... you: when I saw you last; the last time I saw you

to keep body and soul together: make ends meet

lead a... life: (live) a wonderful life

poor I have been: *emphatic structure* = I have been poor

by heaven *(excl)* by God! by Jove! (upon) my word!

that of: the life of

Grammaire au fil des nouvelles

Traduisez les phrases suivantes inspirées du texte (le premier chiffre renvoie à la page, les suivants aux lignes).

Je me suis souvent émerveillé de l'assurance des hommes politiques (prétérit ou présent parfait? *wonder* + ? 54 - 2).

Une fin d'après-midi j'ai entendu sonner (it wasn't early when he heard what? 54 - 28,30).

Il a eu du mal à allumer sa cigarette (*it was difficult for him to light it*, ou: *he had some difficulty...* 56 - 4).

J'espère que vous ne voyez pas d'inconvénient à ce que je vienne ainsi vous rendre visite (would you mind if I opened the window = would you mind ...opening... 56 - 9).

Je viens de lire un de vos livres (temps du verbe? *one of your books*, mais essayons: *a book of...?* 56 - 13).

J'espère que vous n'allez pas trouver bizarre qu'un parfait inconnu vous parle de cette façon (*think, consider, judge etc.* + *it* + *adj.* + *proposition infinitive* introduite par *for*, 56 - 24,25).

Je suis marié depuis 6 ans (*he got married 6 years ago; it's 6 years since he got married* ou bien? 56 - 31).

C'est tout ce qui m'attend pour tout le reste de ma vie (we look back on the past and forward to the future, 58 - 13,14).

Qu'en pense votre femme (58 - 30)?

Bien des années plus tard je me trouvais par hasard à Séville (pensons à *happen* pour traduire l'idée de hasard, 60 - 13).

Je suis là à cause de quelque chose que vous m'avez dit un jour (relatif *which* obligatoire ou Ø possible? 60 - 30,31).

Je n'avais pas la moindre idée de ce dont il parlait (la position de la préposition dans la subordonnée, 62 - 1).

Il portait un sombrero à larges bords (*adj.* composé, 62 - 13).

Vous n'étiez pas marié (l'incrédulité = *surely...* 62 - 20)?

Je ne voudrais pas échanger la vie que j'ai menée ici contre celle de n'importe quel roi au monde (relatif zéro possible ici? *some king? any king?* 64 - 6,7).

The Lotus Eater

Somerset Maugham remembers here the legend in the *Odyssey* about a Mediterranean people who fed on a fruit called the lotus, which had the power to make those who ate it lose all desire to return to their native country.

But, unlike Ulysses, the hero of this modern version of the legend is a very ordinary man, living the ordinary life of an ordinary bank manager in the anonymous megapolis of London. One day, however he went on a very ordinary holiday tour to Italy, and suddenly discovered he could live nowhere else.

The English have long been in love with Italy. In the nineteenth century, Italy was the spiritual home of the Romantic poets, repelled by the evolution of their own country. Over-industrialized and forgetful of the essential human values, it was turning men into soulless machines. But in Italy, men were still men, and beauty was still respected, so that Robert Browning could write nostalgically:

> *Open my heart and you will see*
> *Graved inside of it "Italy"*

While, for his part, Shelley exclaimed:

> *Paradise of exiles, Italy!*

The twentieth century continued this tradition with such writers as E.M. Forster, in his *The Story of the Siren*, and the youthful Aldous Huxley, who paid his homage in *The Little Mexican*, *The Portrait* and *Young Archimedes*.

For much more modest motives than Shelley, our Mr Wilson made up his mind to become a voluntary exile in the Italian paradise. To be able to do so, he conceived an idea that was not at all ordinary...

Most people, the vast majority in fact, lead the lives that circumstances have thrust upon them, and though some repine, looking upon themselves as round pegs in square holes, and think that if things had been different they might have made a much better showing, the greater part accept their lot, if not with serenity, at all events with resignation. They are like tram-cars travelling for ever on the selfsame rails. They go backwards and forwards, backwards and forwards, inevitably, till they can go no longer and then are
10 sold as scrap-iron. It is not often that you find a man who has boldly taken the course of his life into his own hands. When you do, it is worth while having a good look at him.

That was why I was curious to meet Thomas Wilson. It was an interesting and a bold thing he had done. Of course the end was not yet and until the experiment was concluded it was impossible to call it successful. But from what I had heard it seemed he must be an odd sort of fellow and I thought I should like to know him. I had been told he was reserved, but I had a notion that with patience and tact I
20 could persuade him to confide in me. I wanted to hear the facts from his own lips. People exaggerate, they love to romanticize, and I was quite prepared to discover that his story was not nearly so singular as I had been led to believe.

And this impression was confirmed when at last I made his acquaintance. It was on the Piazza in Capri, where I was spending the month of August at a friend's villa, and a little before sunset, when most of the inhabitants, native and foreign, gather together to chat with their friends in the cool
30 of the evening. There is a terrace that overlooks the Bay of Naples, and when the sun sinks slowly into the sea the island of Ischia is silhouetted against a blaze of splendour. It is one

most: note the structure; in a particularizing sense: *most of the people* who live □ **thrust** *(thrust, thrust, thrust)* forced
repine: repent, regret □ **looking upon**: considering □ **round pegs in square holes**: misfits ≠ the right people in the right place
made... showing: been much more successful
lot: fate, destiny □ **resignation**: they are resigned *to leading* such lives □ **tram-cars**: a tramway system □ **travelling**: driving □ **the selfsame**: exactly the same
till: until □ **can go no longer**: cannot go any longer, any more
scrap-iron: ferrous metal objects used as raw material for new objects □ **boldly**: audaciously □ **taken... hands**: made himself responsible for its direction □ **worth while** ≠ a waste of time
I was curious to meet: I looked forward *to meeting*

experiment: attempt to do something new ≠ *experience* (which has been done)
odd: bizarre, strange □ **fellow**: man; creature; *(Am)* guy
know him: get to know him, make his acquaintance
with patience and tact: by being patient and tactful
confide in me: tell me his secret thoughts
from his own lips: in his own words, from his own mouth
romanticize: invent stories that are more romantic than reality
singular: odd, strange □ **led to believe**: induced, made to believe

made his acquaintance: met him, got to know him

at a friend's villa: at the villa belonging to a friend of mine
sunset: dark □ **native**: for whom Italy was their native country
gather together: assemble □ **chat**: have chats □ **cool** ≠ heat
overlooks: looks down over, has a view over
sinks: goes down, sets
silhouetted: outlined □ **blaze**: fire, furnace

of the most lovely sights in the world. I was standing there with my friend and host watching it, when suddenly he said:

"Look, there's Wilson."

"Where?"

"The man sitting on the parapet, with his back to us. He's got a blue shirt on."

I saw an undistinguished back and a small head of grey hair, short and rather thin.

10   "I wish he'd turn round," I said.

"He will presently."

"Ask him to come and have a drink with us at Morgano's."

"All right."

The instant of overwhelming beauty had passed and the sun, like the top of an orange, was dipping into a wine-red sea. We turned round and leaning our backs against the parapet looked at the people who were sauntering to and fro. They were all talking their heads off and the cheerful

20 noise was exhilarating. Then the church bell, rather cracked, but with a fine resonant note, began to ring. The Piazza at Capri, with its clock tower over the footpath that leads up from the harbour, with the church up a flight of steps, is a perfect setting for an opera by Donizetti, and you felt that the voluble crowd might at any moment break out into a rattling chorus. It was charming and unreal.

I was so intent on the scene that I had not noticed Wilson get off the parapet and come towards us. As he passed us my friend stopped him.

30   "Hullo, Wilson, I haven't seen you bathing the last few days."

"I've been bathing on the other side for a change."

70

sights: things worth seeing; to go sightseeing; a sightseer
host: who gives hospitality to a guest

sitting: seated □ **with his back to us**: turning his back towards us
□ **he's got a blue shirt on**: he's wearing a blue shirt
undistinguished: ordinary, nondescript □ **head of grey hair**: grey-haired head □ **rather thin**: a little (too) thin
I wish he'd turn round: expresses regret = if only he would turn round □ **presently**: soon, in a short while
come and have: note *and* after verbs of motion in the imperative mood
all right: I will, agreed
overwhelming: overpowering; he was overwhelmed by the beauty
top ≠ bottom □ **dipping**: sinking, setting □ **wine-red**: as red as wine
leaning: propping, supporting
sauntering: walking idly, strolling □ **to and fro**: up and down
talking their heads off: talking animatedly, twenty to the dozen □
cheerful: happy □ **exhilarating**: exciting, thrilling □ **bell** = *cloche*
cracked: damaged □ **resonant**: resounding □ **ring**: sound, peal
clock tower: tower *(= tour)* with a clock □ **footpath**: lane for pedestrians □ **harbour**: place for boats at anchor □ **flight of steps**
(= escalier) N.B. *steps* when outside; *stairs* when inside □ **setting**:
décor □ **break out into**: suddenly begin (singing)
rattling: noisy □ **chorus**: refrain that people sing together
intent on: attentive to, concentrated on □ **noticed**: seen
passed us: went past us

the last few days: for some days. Note the order of words; the *last (first) five* weeks
for a change: as a change; to make, have a change

My friend then introduced me. Wilson shook hands with me politely, but with indifference; a great many strangers come to Capri for a few days, or a few weeks, and I had no doubt he was constantly meeting people who came and went; and then my friend asked him to come along and have a drink with us.

"I was just going back to supper," he said.

"Can't it wait?" I asked.

"I suppose it can," he smiled.

10   Though his teeth were not very good his smile was attractive. It was gentle and kindly. He was dressed in a blue cotton shirt and a pair of grey trousers, much creased and none too clean, of a thin canvas, and on his feet he wore a pair of very old espadrilles. The get-up was picturesque, and very suitable to the place and the weather, but it did not at all go with his face. It was a lined, long face, deeply sunburned, thin-lipped, with small grey eyes rather close together and tight, neat features. The grey hair was carefully brushed. It was not a plain face, indeed in his youth Wilson

20   might have been good-looking, but a prim one. He wore the blue shirt, open at the neck, and the grey canvas trousers, not as though they belonged to him, but as though, shipwrecked in his pyjamas, he had been fitted out with odd garments by compassionate strangers. Notwithstanding this careless attire he looked like the manager of a branch office in an insurance company, who should by rights be wearing a black coat with pepper-and-salt trousers, a white collar, and an unobjectionable tie. I could very well see myself going to him to claim the insurance money when I

30   had lost a watch, and being rather disconcerted while I answered the questions he put to me by his obvious impression, for all his politeness, that people who made

introduced : said "May I introduce you to my friend" □ **shook hands with me** : shook me by the hand □ **a great many** : very many, a great number of □ **a few days** : some, several days

he was constantly meeting : he kept meeting

asked : invited □ **come along and have** : note *and* have (a drink); note *have* for many everyday events: have a meal, a cup of tea, breakfast, a sleep, etc. □ **to supper** : to have supper

can't it wait : surely it can wait; it can wait, can't it?

I suppose it can : I suppose (imagine) so

teeth : plural of *tooth* □ **smile** = *sourire*

gentle ≠ hard □ **kindly** : kind, good-natured □ **was dressed in** : wore

shirt = *chemise* □ **trousers** *(plur)* : a pair of blue jeans, pyjamas, binoculars, glasses, etc. □ **canvas** : cloth *(= toile)*

get-up : way of dressing, outfit

suitable : appropriate □ **weather** *(U)* it was Ø hot weather □ **did not go with** : did not suit □ **lined** : wrinkled ≠ smooth □ **deeply** : intensely □ **sunburned** : tanned, bronzed □ **thin-lipped** : with thin lips □ **close together** ≠ far apart □ **tight** ≠ relaxed □ **neat** : precise □ **features** : facial traits □ **plain** : unattractive, devoid of attractiveness □ **good-looking** : handsome □ **prim** : stiff, formal, strait-laced □ **neck** = *cou*

belonged to him : were his property, were his

shipwrecked : when his boat was wrecked (i.e. destroyed) □ **fitted out** : supplied, provided □ **odd** : different, not matching □ **garments** : clothes □ **notwithstanding** : in spite of, despite □ **careless** : negligent □ **attire** : outfit □ **branch office** ≠ head office □ **by rights** : normally □ **pepper-and-salt** : (trousers) the colour of pepper and salt □ **unobjectionable** : that no one could object to □ **tie** = *cravate* □ **claim** : ask for

lost *(lose, lost, lost)* ≠ found □ **watch** = *montre* □ **disconcerted** : taken aback, put out, dismayed □ **put to me** : asked me □ **obvious** : evident □ **for** : in spite of, despite

such claims were either fools or knaves.

Moving off, we strolled across the Piazza and down the street till we came to Morgano's. We sat in the garden. Around us people were talking in Russian, German, Italian, and English. We ordered drinks. Donna Lucia, the host's wife, waddled up and in her low, sweet voice passed the time of day with us. Though middle-aged now and portly, she had still traces of the wonderful beauty that thirty years before had driven artists to paint so many bad portraits of 10 her. Her eyes, large and liquid, were the eyes of Hera and her smile was affectionate and gracious. We three gossiped for a while, for there is always a scandal of one sort or another in Capri to make a topic of conversation, but nothing was said of particular interest and in a little while Wilson got up and left us. Soon afterwards we strolled up to my friend's villa to dine. On the way he asked me what I had thought of Wilson.

"Nothing," I said. "I don't believe there's a word of truth in your story."

20   "Why not?"

"He isn't the sort of man to do that sort of thing."

"How does anyone know what anyone is capable of?"

"I should put him down as an absolutely normal man of business who's retired on a comfortable income from gilt-edged securities. I think your story's just the ordinary Capri tittle-tattle."

"Have it your own way," said my friend.

We were in the habit of bathing at a beach called the Baths of Tiberius. We took a fly down the road to a certain 30 point and then wandered through lemon groves and vineyards, noisy with cicadas and heavy with the hot smell of the sun, till we came to the top of the cliff down which

74

fools: idiots □ **knaves**: scoundrels, rogues, swindlers
moving off: going away □ **strolled**: walked slowly, sauntered

talking: chatting, conversing
ordered drinks: orderered (the waiter to bring drinks)
waddled: walked like a duck □ **low**: 1) soft 2) deep □ **passed the time of day**: chatted □ **middle-aged**: neither young nor old □
portly: stout
driven *(drive, drove, driven)*: impelled, incited

affectionate: full of affection □ **gossiped**: exchanged gossip *(U)*, titbits, scandalous items of news
topic: subject
of particular interest: particularly interesting
strolled up: walked up slowly, sauntered up
dine: have dinner □ **on the way**: during the stroll □ **what I had thought of**: what opinion I had formed of (Wilson)
I don't believe there's a word of truth = I believe there's not a word of truth (in your story)
why not?: why don't you?
that sort of thing = those sorts of things. N.B. agreement in number between *sort* and *kind* and the following noun
put him down: consider him □ **man of business**: businessman
retired: gone into retirement □ **income**: revenue □ **gilt-edged securities** = *placements de père de famille*
tittle-tattle: gossip, titbits, scandal-mongering
have it your own way: believe what you like; as you like
were in the habit of: it was a habit of ours (to bathe) □ **beach** = *plage* □ **fly**: small horse-drown carriage
wandered: walked at random, aimlessly □ **lemon groves**: orchards of lemons □ **vineyards**: fields of vines □ **cicadas** = *cigales*
cliff: vertical rock

a steep winding path led to the sea. A day or two later, just before we got down my friend said:

"Oh, there's Wilson back again."

We scrunched over the beach, the only drawback to the bathing-place being that it was shingle and not sand, and as we came along Wilson saw us and waved. He was standing up, a pipe in his mouth, and he wore nothing but a pair of trunks. His body was dark brown, thin but not emaciated, and, considering his wrinkled face and grey hair,
10 youthful. Hot from our walk, we undressed quickly and plunged at once into the water. Six feet from the shore it was thirty feet deep, but so clear that you could see the bottom. It was warm, yet invigorating.

When I got out Wilson was lying on his belly, with a towel under him reading a book. I lit a cigarette and went and sat down beside him.

"Had a nice swim?" he asked.

He put his pipe inside his book to mark the place and closing it put it down on the pebbles beside him. He was
20 evidently willing to talk.

"Lovely", I said. "It's the best bathing in the world."

"Of course people think those were the Baths of Tiberius." He waved his hand towards a shapeless mass of masonry that stood half in the water and half out. "But that's all rot. It was just one of his villas, you know."

I did. But it is just as well to let people tell you things when they want to. It disposes them kindly towards you if you suffer them to impart information. Wilson gave a chuckle.

30 "Funny old fellow, Tiberius. Pity they're saying now there's not a word of truth in all those stories about him."

He began to tell me all about Tiberius. Well, I had read

76

steep : abrupt ≠ gentle □ **winding** : twisting ≠ straight □ **path** : track
got down : climbed down, descended

scrunched : walked making a grating sound □ **drawback** : inconvenience □ **shingle** (uncountable) : small stones on a beach □ **sand** = *sable* □ **waved** : gestured, motioned with his hand
nothing but : nothing except, with the exception of
trunks : for bathing; cf. a pair of shorts, jeans, trousers
wrinkled : full of wrinkles, lined, furrowed
youthful : if not young, which reminds you of youth □ **undressed** : took our clothes off □ **plunged** : dived □ **shore** : land
thirty feet deep : 30 ft in depth. Cf. 6 ft tall; a mile long
invigorating : refreshing, stimulating
belly : front, stomach □ **towel** : cloth to dry yourself
lit *(light, lit, lit)* or *(light, -ed, -ed)* : can you give me a light for my cigarette?
had a nice swim? = (have you) had a nice swim? Cf. other activities: have a bathe, a sail, a walk, a drive, a ride, etc.
pebbles : small round stones you find on the beach or in a river
willing : prepared, ready
bathing : i.e. in general; in particular = *a bathe*. Cf. sailing ≠ a sail; walking ≠ a walk; driving ≠ a drive; riding ≠ a ride
shapeless : formless
masonry : stones placed by a mason
all rot : all nonsense, rubbish □ **one of his villas** : a villa of his
it is just as well : you had better (let people tell...)
disposes them kindly : makes them feel well-disposed
suffer : here = permit, allow □ **impart** : give information *(U)*
chuckle : gentle, soft laugh
funny : strange, odd □ **fellow** : individual, chap □ **pity** = it's a pity
there's not... truth *(emph);* cf. there isn't a word of truth
tell me all about : tell me (the whole story) about

my Suetonius too and I had read histories of the Early Roman Empire, so there was nothing very new to me in what he said. But I observed that he was not ill-read. I remarked on it.

"Oh, well, when I settled down here I was naturally interested and I have plenty of time for reading. When you live in a place like this, with all its associations, it seems to make history so actual. You might almost be living in historical times yourself."

10   I should remark here that this was in 1913. The world was an easy, comfortable place and no one could have imagined that anything might happen seriously to disturb the serenity of existence.

"How long have you been here?" I asked.

"Fifteen years." He gave the blue and placid sea a glance, and a strangely tender smile hovered on his thin lips. "I fell in love with the place at first sight. You've heard, I daresay, of the mythical German who came here on the Naples boat just for lunch and a look at the Blue Grotto and stayed forty
20 years; well, I can't say I exactly did that, but it's come to the same thing in the end. Only it won't be forty years in my case. Twenty-five. Still, that's better than a poke in the eye with a sharp stick."

I waited for him to go on. For what he had just said looked indeed as though there might be something after all in the singular story I had heard. But at that moment my friend came dripping out of the water very proud of himself because he had swum a mile, and the conversation turned to other things.

30   After that I met Wilson several times, either in the Piazza or on the beach. He was amiable and polite. He was always pleased to have a talk and I found out that he not only knew

read *(read, read, read)* : perused □ **early** ≠ late
new to me : unfamiliar to me, strange to me, unknown to me
observed : noticed □ **ill-read** ≠ well-read, widely read; cf. well-travelled = who has travelled a lot □ **remarked** : passed a remark
settled down : came to live permanently, for good

a place like this : such a place as this; this kind of place
actual : real; present N.B. both senses of *actual* possible here
times : days, ages, epochs; the good old days
remark : pass the remark, say
could have imagined : it was impossible for anyone to imagine
happen : occur, take place □ **seriously to disturb** = to disturb seriously
how long have you been here? : since when have you been here?
placid : peaceful, calm □ **glance** : rapid look
hovered : stayed immobile □ **thin** ≠ thick, fleshy □ **lips** = *lèvres*
at first sight : as soon as I saw it, immediately, straight away □
I daresay : I imagine, I suppose, I'm sure
for lunch and a look : to have Ø lunch and a look
it's come to the same thing in the end : the result is the same
in my case : as far as I am concerned
poke : blow, hit
sharp : pointed □ **stick** : piece of wood
waited for him to go on : waited until he continued
looked as though : gave the impression □ **something** : some truth

dripping : with drops of water falling from his wet body
swum *(swim, swam, swum)* **a mile** : had a mile's swim

met *(meet, met, met)* : came across, ran into, had meetings with
amiable : affable, genial, polite, courteous
have a talk : cf. have a look, a bathe, etc.

every inch of the island but also the adjacent mainland. He had read a great deal on all sorts of subjects, but his speciality was the history of Rome and on this he was very well informed. He seemed to have little imagination and to be of no more than average intelligence. He laughed a good deal, but with restraint, and his sense of humour was tickled by simple jokes. A commonplace man. I did not forget the odd remark he had made during the first short chat we had had by ourselves, but he never so much as approached the
10 topic again. One day on our return from the beach, dismissing the cab at the Piazza, my friend and I told the driver to be ready to take us up to Anacapri at five. We were going to climb Monte Solaro, dine at a tavern we favoured, and walk down in the moonlight. For it was full moon and the views by night were lovely. Wilson was standing by while we gave the cabman instructions, for we had given him a lift to save him the hot dusty walk, and more from politeness than for any other reason I asked him if he would care to join us.
20 "It's my party," I said.

"I'll come with pleasure," he answered.

But when the time came to set out my friend was not feeling well, he thought he had stayed too long in the water, and would not face the long and tiring walk. So I went alone with Wilson. We climbed the mountain, admired the spacious view, and got back to the inn as night was falling, hot, hungry, and thirsty. We had ordered our dinner beforehand. The food was good, for Antonio was an excellent cook, and the wine came from his own vineyard.
30 It was so light that you felt you could drink it like water and we finished the first bottle with our macaroni. By the time we had finished the second we felt that there was nothing

80

every inch : the smallest detail □ **mainland** ≠ island

a great deal : widely □ **all sorts of subjects :** every sort of subject

on this... informed *(emphatic structure)* = this was something he was very well informed on □ **little imagination :** not very much imagination □ **to be of... intelligence :** to have no more than average intelligence □ **tickled :** stimulated

jokes : comic stories □ **commonplace :** banal, ordinary

odd : bizarre, strange □ **chat :** talk, conversation

so much as approached the topic : even touched on the subject

on our return : when we returned

dismissing the cab : telling the taxi driver to go away

ready : prepared, on time

climb : go up, ascend □ **favoured :** liked, preferred

it was Ø full moon : note the zero article

standing by : standing (near) by

cabman : taxi driver □ **given him a lift :** taken him with us in our taxi □ **save him the hot, dusty walk :** avoid him walking in the heat and in the dust □ **politeness :** courtesy

care to join us : like to be one of the party

when the time came : when it was time □ **set out :** leave, go away

would not face : refused to contemplate □ **tiring :** fatiguing

inn : tavern □ **Ø night was falling :** the sun was setting; note the zero article

beforehand : in advance, previously □ **food :** cooking

vineyard : where vines grow to make wine

like water : as if it were water

macaroni *(sing)* : the macaroni was good but the spaghetti was even better □ **by the time :** when; before

81

much wrong with life. We sat in a little garden under a great vine laden with grapes. The air was exquisitely soft. The night was still and we were alone. The maid brought us *bel paese* cheese and a plate of figs. I ordered coffee and strega, which is the best liqueur they make in Italy. Wilson would not have a cigar, but lit his pipe.

"We've got plenty of time before we need start," he said, "the moon won't be over the hill for another hour."

"Moon or no moon," I said briskly, "of course we've got
10 plenty of time. That's one of the delights of Capri, that there's never any hurry."

"Leisure," he said. "If people only knew! It's the most priceless thing a man can have and they're such fools they don't even know it's something to aim at. Work? They work for work's sake. They haven't got the brains to realize that the only object of work is to obtain leisure."

Wine has the effect on some people of making them indulge in general reflections. These remarks were true, but no one could have claimed that they were original. I did not
20 say anything, but struck a match to light my cigar.

"It was full moon the first time I came to Capri," he went on reflectively. "It might be the same moon as tonight."

"It was, you know," I smiled.

He grinned. The only light in the garden was what came from an oil lamp that hung over our heads. It had been scanty to eat by, but it was good now for confidences.

"I didn't mean that. I mean, it might be yesterday. Fifteen years it is, and when I look back it seems like a month. I'd never been to Italy before. I came for my summer holiday.
30 I went to Naples by boat from Marseilles and I had a look round, Pompeii, you know, and Paestum and one or two places like that; then I came here for a week. I liked the look

82

there was nothing much wrong with life : life was all right
laden : hanging □ **grapes :** the fruit of the vine □ **soft :** mild, gentle
still : silent; motionless □ **maid :** servant □ **brought** *(bring, brought, brought)* carried □ **cheese** = *fromage* □ **figs** = *figues*
liqueur ∅ they make : liqueur (that) they make i.e. zero relative
lit *(light, lit, lit)* : put a match to (his pipe)
we need start : we need to start (infinitive with or without *to*)
over the hill : on the other side of the hill
briskly : energetically
delights : joys, great pleasures, delightful aspects
hurry : precipitation, hustle, rush
leisure : spare time ≠ work (3 uncountable nouns)
priceless : inestimable, invaluable □ **fools :** idiots
to aim at : at which we can aim; to have as an aim, object, end
for work's sake : for the love of work □ **brains :** intelligence
object : aim, target, end

indulge in : take pleasure in
claimed : said, declared, maintained
struck *(strike, struck, struck)* □ **a match :** lit a match

reflectively : pensively, thoughtfully □ **it might be :** it could be

grinned : smiled widely; gave a broad grin
oil lamp ≠ electric lamp □ **hung** *(hang, hung, hung)* : was suspended
scanty : insufficient □ **to eat by :** (for us) to eat by
I didn't mean that : that wasn't what I meant
look back : i.e. into the past □ **like a month :** as if it were a month

I had a look round : I looked round; visited the sights; did some sight-seeing
like that : such as that

of the place right away, from the sea, I mean, as I watched it come closer and closer; and then when we got into the little boats from the steamer and landed at the quay, with all that crowd of jabbering people who wanted to take your luggage, and the hotel touts, and the tumbledown houses on the Marina and the walk up to the hotel, and dining on the terrace —well, it just got me. That's the truth. I didn't know if I was standing on my head or my heels. I'd never drunk Capri wine before, but I'd heard of it; I think I must
10 have got a bit tight. I sat on that terrace after they'd all gone to bed and watched the moon over the sea, and there was Vesuvius with a great red plume of smoke rising up from it. Of course I know now that wine I drank was ink, Capri wine my eye, but I thought it all right then. But it wasn't the wine that made me drunk, it was the shape of the island and those jabbering people, the moon and the sea and the oleander in the hotel garden. I'd never seen an oleander before."

It was a long speech and it had made him thirsty. He took up his glass, but it was empty. I asked him if he would have
20 another strega.

"It's sickly stuff. Let's have a bottle of wine. That's sound, that is, pure juice of the grape and can't hurt anyone."

I ordered more wine, and when it came filled the glasses. He took a long drink and after a sigh of pleasure went on.

"Next day I found my way to the bathing-place we go to. Not bad bathing, I thought. Then I wandered about the island. As luck would have it, there was a *festa* up at the Punta di Timberio and I ran straight into the middle of it.
30 An image of the Virgin and priests, acolytes swinging censers, and a whole crowd of jolly, laughing, excited

84

right away : immediately, straight away

closer and closer : nearer and nearer

steamer : boat worked by steam □ **landed** : got off the boat □ **quay** : jetty □ **jabbering** : chattering incomprehensibly

luggage *(U)* : baggage □ **hotel touts** : employees who try to make you choose their hotel □ **tumbledown** : decrepit, shabby

got me : charmed me; got me under its spell, charm □ **I didn't know... heels** : I was dazed, in a daze

I'd heard of it : I'd heard (people talk) of it

tight : drunk, tipsy, intoxicated

over the sea : above the sea

smoke : dark and visible gas from a fire □ **rising** *(rise, rose, risen)* : coming up □ **ink** = *encre*

my eye : I don't believe it; my foot □ **all right** : quite good

drunk : tight, tipsy □ **shape** : form, contours

oleander = *laurier-rose*

I'd never... before : it was the first time I had seen an oleander

made him thirsty : made him want a drink

another strega : one more strega

sickly stuff : an over-sweet drink (*stuff* can substitute for any object)

hurt anyone : harm anyone; do harm to anyone

took a long drink : drank a large quantity, took a large draught □ **went on** : continued □ **bathing-place we go to** : bathing-place (that) we go to □ **wandered about** : rambled aimlessly, strolled at random

as luck would have it : by chance (lucky or unlucky)

ran straight into the middle : found myself in the centre

swinging *(swing, swung, swung)* □ **censers** : making censers (= *encensoirs*) go back and forward □ **jolly** : cheerful, joyful, merry

people, a lot of them all dressed up. I ran across an Englishman there and asked him what it was all about. "Oh, it's the feast of the Assumption," he said, "at least that's what the Catholic Church says it is, but that's just their hanky-panky. It's the festival of Venus. Pagan, you know. Aphrodite rising from the sea and all that." It gave me quite a funny feeling to hear him. It seemed to take one a long way back, if you know what I mean. After that I went down one night to have a look at the Faraglioni by moonlight. If
10 the fates had wanted me to go on being a bank manager they oughtn't to have let me take that walk."

"You were a bank manager, were you?" I asked.

I had been wrong about him, but not far wrong.

"Yes. I was manager of the Crawford Street branch of the York and City. It was convenient for me because I lived up Hendon way. I could get from door to door in thirty-seven minutes."

He puffed at his pipe and relit it.

"That was my last night, that was. I'd got to be back at
20 the bank on Monday morning. When I looked at those two great rocks sticking out of the water, with the moon above them, and all the little lights of the fishermen in their boats catching cuttlefish, all so peaceful and beautiful, I said to myself, well, after all, why should I go back? It wasn't as if I had anyone dependent on me. My wife had died of bronchial pneumonia four years before and the kid went to live with her grandmother, my wife's mother. She was an old fool, she didn't look after the kid properly and she got blood-poisoning, they amputated her leg, but they couldn't
30 save her and she died, poor little thing."

"How terrible," I said.

"Yes, I was cut up at the time, though of course not so

dressed up : disguised, in fancy dress □ **ran across** : came across, ran into □ **what it was all about** : what was the reason for all this **feast** : holy day ≠ festival (= a non-Christian ceremony)

hanky-panky : nonsense; fuss; eye-wash □ **pagan** : non-Christian **rising** *(rise, rose, risen)* : coming up □ **quite a funny feeling** : rather a strange impression □ **take one a long way back** : make sb go back in time to a very distant epoch

the fates : the goddesses of destiny □ **bank manager** : man in charge of the day-to-day running (managing) of a bank
you were... were you? : non-negative tag question, which means that the speaker is absolutely sure of what he says, but would like more details □ **far wrong** : greatly mistaken
convenient : suitable, handy □ **up Hendon way** : in the direction of Hendon □ **get from door to door** : commute; he was a commuter

puffed : sucked (in order to produce puffs of smoke) □ **at** : denotes unsuccessful effort □ **relit it** : lit it again □ **I'd got to be** : I had to be, I was obliged to be
great : enormous, huge; impressive □ **sticking** (out of) : projecting **fishermen** : men who caught fish for their living
catching *(catch, caught, caught)* : taking □ **cuttlefish** = *seiches*
why should I go back? : why go back? Note the *should* after *why*
anyone dependent on me : who depended on me; any dependant □
had died... before : i.e. she was now dead □ **kid** *(fam)* : child

fool : idiot □ **look after** : care for, pay attention to □ **properly** : as she ought to have done □ **blood-poisoning** : infection of the blood **save her** : prevent her from dying
how terrible : what a terrible thing
cut up *(fam)* : distressed, grief-stricken

much as if the kid had been living with me, but I dare say it was a mercy. Not much chance for a girl with only one leg. I was sorry about my wife too. We got on very well together. Though I don't know if it would have continued. She was the sort of woman who was always bothering about what other people'd think. She didn't like travelling. Eastbourne was her idea of a holiday. D'you know, I'd never crossed the Channel till after her death."

"But I suppose you've got other relations, haven't
10 you?"

"None. I was an only child. My father had a brother, but he went to Australia before I was born. I don't think anyone could easily be more alone in the world than I am. There wasn't any reason I could see why I shouldn't do exactly what I wanted. I was thirty-four at that time."

He had told me he had been on the island for fifteen years. That would make him forty-nine. Just about the age I should have given him.

"I'd been working since I was seventeen. All I had to look
20 forward to was doing the same old thing day after day till I retired on my pension. I said to myself, is it worth it? What's wrong with chucking it all up and spending the rest of my life down here? It was the most beautiful place I'd ever seen. But I'd had a business training, I was cautious by nature. "No", I said, "I won't be carried away like this, I'll go tomorrow like I said I would and think it over. Perhaps when I get back to London I'll think quite differently." Damned fool, wasn't I? I lost a whole year that way."

"You didn't change your mind, then?
30 "You bet I didn't. All the time I was working I kept thinking of the bathing here and the vineyards and the walks over the hills and the moon and the sea, and the

88

had been living: note the verbal form = durative & imperfective aspect □ **mercy**: clemency, grace, blessing □ **chance**: hope **leg** = *jambe* □ **sorry**: sad □ **wife** ≠ husband □ **we got on very well**: we were on very good terms; we rarely disagreed or quarrelled **she was always bothering**: she kept worrying, feeling concerned **what people'd think**: how people would react; people's opinions

crossed: gone across □ **never... till after her death**: until she died; before she died □ **relations**: family, relatives

an only child: with no brothers or sisters **before I was born**: before my birth

reason... why I shouldn't do: reason for my not doing **thirty-four**: 34 years old, of age; a man of thirty-four **he had been... for 15 years**: he had come... 15 years ago; it was 15 years since he had come. Note the tenses!

I'd... since I was 17: I'd... since (the time when) I was 17; since the age of 17 □ **look forward to**: hope for **retired**: went into retirement; was pensioned off □ **is it worth it?**: is it worth while? does it pay? □ **what's wrong with chucking it all up?**: why not drop everything? **training**: qualification and experience □ **cautious**: prudent **carried away**: completely under the influence of my emotions; lose my self-control □ **think it over**: reflect carefully on it **think quite differently**: have a completely different viewpoint **damned fool**: utter (complete) idiot □ **that way**: like that **change your mind**: think differently; change your opinion **you bet**: you can be sure, certainly not □ **kept thinking**: continued to think, kept on thinking □ **bathing**: sea-bathing **walks**: rambles, hikes, wandering

Piazza in the evening when everyone walks about for a bit of a chat after the day's work is over. There was only one thing that bothered me: I wasn't sure if I was justified in not working like everybody else did. Then I read a sort of history book, by a man called Marion Crawford it was, and there was a story about Sybaris and Crotona. There were two cities; and in Sybaris they just enjoyed life and had a good time, and in Crotona they were hardy and industrious and all that. And one day the men of Crotona came over
10 and wiped Sybaris out, and then after a while a lot of other fellows came over from somewhere else and wiped Crotona out. Nothing remains of Sybaris, not a stone, and all that's left of Crotona is just one column. That settled the matter for me."

"Oh?"

"It came to the same in the end, didn't it? And when you look back now, who were the mugs?"

I did not reply and he went on.

"The money was rather a bother. The bank didn't
20 pension one off till after thirty years' service, but if you retired before that they gave you a gratuity. With that and what I'd got for the sale of my house and the little I'd managed to save, I just hadn't enough to buy an annuity to last the rest of my life. It would have been silly to sacrifice everything so as to lead a pleasant life and not have a sufficient income to make it pleasant. I wanted to have a little place of my own, a servant to look after me, enough to buy tobacco, decent food, books now and then, and something over for emergencies. I knew pretty well how
30 much I needed. I found I had just enough to buy an annuity for twenty-five years."

"You were thirty-five at the time?"

walks about : strolls, saunters around (here and here) □ **a bit of a chat** : a bit of Ø conversation □ **the day's work** : cf. in a year's time □ **over** : finished □ **bothered** : worried □ **justified** : morally right

by... it was : *emphatic order of words* = it was by a man...

enjoyed life : enjoyed themselves in life □ **had a good time** : enjoyed themselves □ **hardy** : vigorous □ **industrious** : hard-working

wiped... out : destroyed completely □ **a while** : a certain time **fellows** *(fam)* : men, chaps □ **somewhere else** : another part of the world □ **nothing remains** : there is nothing left **settled the matter** : solved the problem

it came to the same : it made no difference
look back : remember things; look back in time □ **mugs** : dupes, saps □ **went on** : continued; resumed
rather a bother : quite a worry, rather a problem
pension one off : let one retire on a pension □ **30 years' service** *(genitive of duration)* : cf. the day's work □ **gratuity** : sum of money **got for the sale of my house** : obtained (in return) for selling...
managed to save : succeeded in economizing □ **annuity** : contract to be paid an annual sum of money □ **silly** : idiotic, foolish **so as to** : in order to □ **a sufficient income** : enough revenue **a little place of my own** : a small house that belonged to me **look after me** : take care of me
now and then : from time to time
something over : something (left) over □ **emergencies** : urgent cases □ **pretty well** : quite well
for twenty-five years : over a twenty-five-year period
at the time : at that period

91

"Yes. It would carry me on till I was sixty. After all, no one can be certain of living longer than that, a lot of men die in their fifties, and by the time a man's sixty he's had the best of life."

"On the other hand no one can be sure of dying at sixty," I said.

"Well, I don't know. It depends on himself, doesn't it?"

"In your place I should have stayed on at the bank till I was entitled to my pension."

10 "I should have been forty-seven then. I shouldn't have been too old to enjoy my life here, I'm older than that now and I enjoy it as much as I ever did, but I should have been too old to experience the particular pleasure of a young man. You know, you can have just as good a time at fifty as you can at thirty, but it's not the same sort of good time. I wanted to live the perfect life while I still had the energy and the spirit to make the most of it. Twenty-five years seemed a long time to me, and twenty-five years of happiness seemed worth paying something pretty substan-
20 tial for. I'd made up my mind to wait a year and I waited a year. Then I sent in my resignation and as soon as they paid me my gratuity I bought the annuity and came on here."

"An annuity for twenty-five years?"

"That's right."

"Have you never regretted?"

"Never. I've had my money's worth already. And I've got ten years more. Don't you think after twenty-five years of perfect happiness one ought to be satisfied to call it a day?"

30 "Perhaps."

He did not say in so many words what he would do then, but his intention was clear. It was pretty much the story my

92

carry me on: be enough for me, last me
certain of living: sure of living; sure (certain) to live
in their fifties: between the ages of 50 and 60 ☐ **by**: before

on the other hand: (taking it) from another point of view

it depends on himself: note the preposition
in your place: if I had been you (in your shoes) ☐ **till**: until
was entitled to: had the right to, could claim (my pension)
forty-seven: 47 years old, 47 years of age
enjoy it: have (take) pleasure in it
as much as I ever did: as much as I did at any time
experience: feel ☐ **particular**: special
have as good a time: enjoy yourself

had the energy: was energetic enough
spirit: mind; mood ☐ **make the most of it**: benefit best from it

worth paying... for: good enough for me to pay... (in exchange) for
☐ **pretty substantial**: fairly important ☐ **made up my mind**: decided
sent in my resignation: resigned ☐ **paid me my gratuity**: gave me
my lump sum
for 25 years: for (a future period of) 25 years

regretted: been sorry, had remorse, had second thoughts
my money's worth: value for my money
ten years more: another 10 years
ought to be satisfied: should be content ☐ **call it a day**: end
everything i.e. commit suicide

in so many words: explicitly, directly in words
his intention was clear: what he intended (doing) was obvious

friend had told me, but it sounded different when I heard it from his own lips. I stole a glance at him. There was nothing about him that was not ordinary. No one, looking at that neat, prim face, could have thought him capable of an unconventional action. I did not blame him. It was his own life that he had arranged in this strange manner, and I did not see why he should not do what he liked with it. Still, I could not prevent the little shiver that ran down my spine.

10   "Getting chilly?" he smiled. "We might as well start walking down. The moon'll be up by now."

Before we parted Wilson asked me if I would like to go and see his house one day; and two or three days later, finding out where he lived, I strolled up to see him. It was a peasant's cottage, well away from the town, in a vineyard, with a view of the sea. By the side of the door grew a great oleander in full flower. There were only two small rooms, a tiny kitchen, and a lean-to in which fire-wood could be kept. The bedroom was furnished like a monk's cell, but the

20 sitting-room, smelling agreeably of tobacco, was comfortable enough, with two large arm-chairs that he had brought from England, a large roll-top desk, a cottage piano, and crowded bookshelves. On the walls were framed engravings of pictures by G.F. Watts and Lord Leighton. Wilson told me that the house belonged to the owner of the vineyard who lived in another cottage higher up the hill, and his wife came in every day to do the rooms and the cooking. He had found the place on his first visit to Capri, and taking it on his return for good had been there ever since. Seeing the

30 piano and music open on it, I asked him if he would play.

"I'm no good, you know, but I've always been fond of music and I get a lot of fun out of strumming."

sounded : seemed (from what I heard); cf. it looked different (from what I *saw*); it *felt* strange (from what I *felt*) □ **stole** *(steal, stole, stolen)* **a glance** : looked briefly and furtively
neat : tidy, precise □ **prim** : conventional, formal; stiff, prudish
blame : reproach (him *for/with* doing...)

did not see why he should : saw no reason why he should...
prevent : stop, avoid □ **shiver** : tremble; quiver □ **ran down my spine** : descended my back (my backbone)
getting chilly? (is it) becoming (growing) cold? □ **we might as well start** : it would be advisable for us to begin
parted : separated, went our separate ways □ **go and see** : note *and* after *come* and *go* when there is strong intentionality (i.e. future & especially imperative mood) □ **strolled** : walked leisurely
a peasant's cottage : a small house like a small farmer's one
grew *(grow, grew, grown)* : was planted □ **great** : majestic, imposing
oleander = *laurier-rose* □ **in full flower** : in full bloom, blossom
tiny : very small, minute □ **lean-to** : small edifice built against the wall of a larger building □ **fire-wood** : kindling (wood) □ **monk** : man who lives in a monastery □ **smelling of tobacco** : note how a noun is introduced; compare : *it smelled good; he sounded pleasant; he sounded like a pleasant fellow* □ **roll-top desk** = *bureau à cylindre*
crowded : full □ **framed** : in frames □ **engravings** : engraved pictures: prints □ **by** : (done) by ≠ *of* (= depicting)
belonged to : were the property of □ **owner** : proprietor

do the rooms and the cooking : clean and prepare the meals
taking it : renting it □ **on his return** : when he returned
for good : permanently, on a permanent basis □ **ever since** : all the time since; ever since that time □ **no good** = not good (at it); cf. he's no fun = he's not amusing □ **fond of** : keen on
fun : amusement □ **strumming** : amateurish playing

95

He sat down at the piano and played one of the movements from a Beethoven sonata. He did not play very well. I looked at his music, Schumann and Schubert, Beethoven, Bach, and Chopin. On the table on which he had his meals was a greasy pack of cards. I asked him if he played patience.

"A lot."

From what I saw of him then and from what I heard from other people I made for myself what I think must have been
10 a fairly accurate picture of the life he had led for the last fifteen years. It was certainly a very harmless one. He bathed; he walked a great deal, and he seemed never to lose his sense of the beauty of the island which he knew so intimately; he played the piano and he played patience; he read. When he was asked to a party he went and, though a trifle dull, was agreeable. He was not affronted if he was neglected. He liked people, but with an aloofness that prevented intimacy. He lived thriftily, but with sufficient comfort. He never owed a penny. I imagine he had never
20 been a man whom sex had greatly troubled, and if in his younger days he had had now and then a passing affair with a visitor to the island whose head was turned by the atmosphere, his emotion, while it lasted, remained, I am pretty sure, well under his control. I think he was determined that nothing should interfere with his independence of spirit. His only passion was for the beauty of nature, and he sought felicity in the simple and natural things that life offers to everyone. You may say that it was a grossly selfish existence. It was. He was of no use to
30 anybody, but on the other hand he did nobody any harm. His only object was his own happiness, and it looked as though he had attained it. Very few people know where to

at the piano: at the keyboard
from: (extracted) from; an extract □ **did not play very well:** did not perform very well; was not a very good player (performer)

greasy: oily (from being much handled) □ **pack of cards:** set of (playing) cards □ **played Ø patience:** played by himself (note the zero article before games: *play Ø football, rugby, handball,* etc. □ **a lot:** a great deal □ **what I saw of him:** the occasions when I saw him; do you see a lot of each other □ **heard from... people:** heard... people saying □ **fairly accurate:** more or less precise □ **life... led:** life... lived □ **for... 15 years:** since he had come there 15 years ago □ **harmless:** innocent (≠ harmful); it harmed (hurt) no one; it did no one any harm □ **sense:** consciousness, awareness; appreciation **played the piano... Ø patience:** note *the* before musical instruments and Ø before games □ **asked:** invited
a trifle: rather, somewhat, a little □ **affronted:** offended
aloofness: distance, coolness
prevented intimacy: prevented people (from) being intimate with him □ **thriftily:** economically □ **owed a penny:** had the smallest debt □ **troubled:** disturbed; affected; worried
now and then: from time to time □ **passing** ≠ permanent, serious
whose Ø head was turned: who had been greatly affected
while it lasted: as long as it lasted
well under his control: well-controlled; under his self-control □ **was determined:** had decided □ **should:** must; was to. Note the frequent presence of *should* after a verb denoting coercion
sought *(seek, sought, sought)* □ **felicity:** looked for happiness

grossly: extremely; excessively □ **selfish:** egoistic(al) □ **of no use:** useless □ **on the other hand:** from another point of view □ **did nobody any harm:** harmed no one □ **object:** ambition, aim, target
attained: achieved, reached

97

look for happiness; fewer still find it. I don't know whether he was a fool or a wise man. He was certainly a man who knew his own mind. The odd thing about him to me was that he was so immensely commonplace. I should never have given him a second thought but for what I knew, that on a certain day, ten years from then, unless a chance illness cut the thread before, he must deliberately take leave of the world he loved so well. I wondered whether it was the thought of this, never quite absent from his mind, that gave
10 him the peculiar zest with which he enjoyed every moment of the day.

I should do him an injustice if I omitted to state that he was not at all in the habit of talking about himself. I think the friend I was staying with was the only person in whom he had confided. I believe he only told me the story because he suspected I already knew it, and on the evening on which he told it me he had drunk a good deal of wine.

My visit drew to a close and I left the island. The year after, war broke out. A number of things happened to me,
20 so that the course of my life was greatly altered, and it was thirteen years before I went to Capri again. My friend had been back some time, but he was no longer so well off, and had moved into a house that had no room for me; so I was putting up at the hotel. He came to meet me at the boat and we dined together. During dinner I asked him where exactly his house was.

"You know it," he answered. "It's the little place Wilson had. I've built on a room and made it quite nice."

With so many other things to occupy my mind I had not
30 given Wilson a thought for years; but now, with a little shock, I remembered. The ten years he had before him when I made his acquaintance must have elapsed long ago.

look for : seek □ **fewer still** : even fewer people
fool : foolish, thoughtless person □ **wise man** : philosopher
knew his own mind : was sure of what he wanted □ **odd** : strange
commonplace : banal, ordinary; a commonplace □ **never... thought** :
have forgotten him immediately □ **but** : except
10 years from then : in 10 year's time □ **chance illness** : fact of falling
ill by chance □ **the thread** = *le fil* (of life) □ **take leave of** : say
goodbye to □ **world Ø he loved** : note the zero relative
absent from his mind : far from his thoughts
zest : enthusiasm, vigour □ **enjoyed** : took (found) pleasure in

do him an injustice : be unjust towards him □ **omitted** : neglected
□ **state** : say, declare □ **was... in the habit of** : didn't usually (talk)
the friend Ø I was staying with : note zero relative (= the friend *with
whom... in whom...* confided *whom/Ø* he had confided *in*)
suspected : had a suspicion
drunk *(drink, drank, drunk)* **a good deal** : had a lot (of wine)
drew *(draw, drew, drawn)* **to a close** : ended, came to an end
war : armed conflict □ **broke out** : began; an outbreak of fighting
course : direction □ **altered** : changed (for better or for worse) □
it was 13 years before... again : I didn't go back to Capri for
(another) 13 years □ **had been back some time** : had come back
some time before □ **moved into** : settled in □ **no room** : not enough
room □ **putting up** : staying, living (with friends or at a hotel)
dined : had dinner

place Ø Wilson had : the house that/Ø Wilson had (zero relative)
built on a room : added a room (note difference in sense with the
uncountable *room* of line 23) □ **made it quite nice** : altered it into
something quite pleasant □ **had not given Wilson a thought** : had
forgotten (all about) Wilson
must have elapsed : had very probably (almost certainly) ended

"Did he commit suicide as he said he would?"

"It's rather a grim story."

Wilson's plan was all right. There was only one flaw in it and this, I suppose, he could not have foreseen. It had never occurred to him that after twenty-five years of complete happiness, in this quiet backwater, with nothing in the world to disturb his serenity, his character would gradually lose its strength. The will needs obstacles in order to exercise its power; when it is never thwarted, when no
10 effort is needed to achieve one's desires, because one has placed one's desires only in the things that can be obtained by stretching out one's hand, the will grows impotent. If you walk on a level all the time the muscles you need to climb a mountain will atrophy. These observations are trite, but there they are. When Wilson's annuity expired he had no longer the resolution to make the end which was the price he had agreed to pay for that long period of happy tranquillity. I do not think, as far as I could gather, both from what my friend told me and afterwards from others,
20 that he wanted courage. It was just that he couldn't make up his mind. He put it off from day to day.

He had lived on the island for so long and had always settled his accounts so punctually that it was easy for him to get credit; never having borrowed money before, he found a number of people who were willing to lend him small sums when now he asked for them. He had paid his rent regularly for so many years that his landlord, whose wife Assunta still acted as his servant, was content to let things slide for several months. Everyone believed him when he said that a relative
30 had died and that he was temporarily embarrassed because owing to legal formalities he could not for some time get the money that was due to him. He managed to

100

commit suicide: take his own life

rather a grim story: a somewhat unpleasant, cruel, gruesome story

flaw: imperfection

this... foreseen *(emph)*: he couldn't have predicted this □ **it had never occurred to him**: he had never imagined, supposed

backwater: peaceful place, cut off from the mainstream of life

disturb: trouble, upset, risk destroying

lose *(lost, lost)* **its strength**: grow less strong □ **will** = *volonté*

thwarted: obstructed, denied

achieve: realise, make (one's desires) come true

stretching out: reaching out □ **grows impotent**: becomes powerless

on a level: on the flat ≠ uphill, up a hill □ **climb**: go up

atrophy: waste away tend to disappear □ **trite**: banal, commonplace □ **there they are**: I present them nevertheless □ **expired**: came to an end, reached the date of expiry □ **resolution**: determination, will □ **pay for**: pay (in exchange) for. Note: pay the waiter *for* a meal; cf. pay the bill *(for* the meal) □ **as far as I could gather**: from what I could deduce; cf. *as far as I know :* within the limits of my knowledge □ **wanted**: hadn't enough, lacked; was lacking in □ **make up his mind**: decide □ **put if off**: postponed it □ **from day to day**: from one day to the next

settled his accounts: paid his bills (see 1. 17) □ **punctually**: on time, without delay, *(fam)* on the dot □ **borrowed**: asked for money on a temporary basis □ **willing**: ready □ **lend**: give money temporarily

paid his rent: paid the landlord *for* the use of his house

whose ∅ wife: note the zero article

acted as: played the role of □ **let things slide**: do nothing, allow things to take their own course, let things be □ **relative**: relation, member of the family □ **temporarily**: for the time being

owing to: because of, due to □ **for** (introducing duration)

managed: succeeded (in doing), contrived (to do)

hang on after this fashion for something over a year. Then he could get no more credit from the local tradesmen, and there was no one to lend him any more money. His landlord gave him notice to leave the house unless he paid up the arrears of rent before a certain date.

The day before this he went into his tiny bedroom, closed the door and the window, drew the curtain, and lit a brazier of charcoal. Next morning when Assunta came to make his breakfast she found him insensible but still alive. The room
10 was draughty, and though he had done this and that to keep out the fresh air he had not done it very thoroughly. It almost looked as though at the last moment, and desperate though his situation was, he had suffered from a certain infirmity of purpose. Wilson was taken to the hospital, and though very ill for some time he at last recovered. But as a result either of the charcoal poisoning or of the shock he was no longer in complete possession of his faculties. He was not insane, at all events not insane enough to be put in an asylum, but he was quite obviously no longer in his right
20 mind.

"I went to see him," said my friend. "I tried to get him to talk, but he kept looking at me in a funny sort of way, as though he couldn't quite make out where he'd seen me before. He looked rather awful lying there in bed, with a week's growth of grey beard on his chin but except for that funny look in his eyes he seemed quite normal."

"What funny look in his eyes?"

"I don't know exactly how to describe it. Puzzled. It's an absurd comparison, but suppose you threw a stone into the
30 air and it didn't come down but just stayed there..."

"It would be rather bewildering," I smiled.

102

hang on : persevere ☐ **fashion** : manner ☐ **something over** : a little more ☐ **tradesmen** : here = shopkeepers

no one to lend : no one who would lend ☐ **his landlord** : the owner of his house ☐ **gave him notice** : warned him (formally)

arrears of rent : money owed for the occupation of the house

tiny : exiguous; so small you couldn't swing a cat in it

drew : closed, shut ☐ **curtain** = *rideau* ☐ **brazier** = *brasero*

charcoal : wood partly burned without contact with the air

insensible : unconscious, without consciousness ☐ **alive** ≠ dead

draughty : full of draughts ≠ airtight

thoroughly : methodically, meticulously, painstakingly

desperate though the situation was *(emph)* : though the situation was desperate

infirmity of purpose : irresolution, lack of determination; he was not purposeful enough ☐ **recovered** : got well, made a recovery

as a result : note the indefinite article; cf. as a consequence

insane : mad, crazy ☐ **at all events** : at least, in any case

asylum : here = institution for lunatics ☐ **obviously** : evidently ☐

in his right mind : sane, compos mentis

get him to talk : persuade him to talk

kept : continued, went on ☐ **funny sort of way** : strange kind of manner ☐ **make out** : distinguish, understand

rather awful : pretty dreadful

a week's growth of beard : a beard (stubble) that had been growing for a week i.e. genitive of duration ☐ **chin** = *menton*

look in his eyes : way of looking at you, expression in his eyes

puzzled : mystified, perplexed, bewildered

suppose you threw : assume (that) you hurled; it's as though you threw ☐ **come down** : descend, fall down

rather bewildering : a little puzzling, perplexing

"Well, that's the sort of look he had."

It was difficult to know what to do with him. He had no money and no means of getting any. His effects were sold, but for too little to pay what he owed. He was English, and the Italian authorities did not wish to make themselves responsible for him. The British Consul in Naples had no funds to deal with the case. He could of course be sent back to England, but no one seemed to know what could be done with him when he got there. Then Assunta, the servant, said
10 that he had been a good master and a good tenant, and as long as he had the money had paid his way; he could sleep in the woodshed in the cottage in which she and her husband lived, and he could share their meals. This was suggested to him. It was difficult to know whether he understood or not. When Assunta came to take him from the hospital he went with her without remark. He seemed to have no longer a will of his own. She had been keeping him now for two years.

"It's not very comfortable, you know," said my friend.
20 "They've rigged him up a ramshackle bed and given him a couple of blankets, but there's no window, and it's icy cold in winter and like an oven in summer. And the food's pretty rough. You know how these peasants eat: macaroni on Sundays and meat once in a blue moon."

"What does he do with himself all the time?"

"He wanders about the hills. I've tried to see him two or three times, but it's no good; when he sees you coming he runs like a hare. Assunta comes down to have a chat with me now and then and I give her a bit of money so that she
30 can buy him tobacco, but God knows if he ever gets it."

"Do they treat him all right?" I asked.

"I'm sure Assunta's kind enough. She treats him like a

the sort of look he had: how he looked
what to do: what one could do
means: way, possibility □ **any**: any (money) □ **effects**: possessions
for = in exchange for □ **what he owed**: his debts

fund: money □ **deal with**: settle, solve; cope with
know what could be done: know what to do

master: employer □ **tenant**: occupant of a rented house
the money: here = enough money □ **paid his way** ≠ go into debt
woodshed: small building where the firewood is stocked
share their meals: eat with them
it was difficult to know: people had (great) difficulty (in) knowing;
it wasn't easy (for people) to know
without remark: without making a remark, without a comment
a will of his own *(emph structure)*: his own will □ **she had been
keeping him now for 2 years**: she has started looking after him 2
years ago; it was 2 years since she had started keeping him
rigged (him) up: improvised (for him) □ **ramshackle**: tumbledown
blankets = *couvertures* □ **icy cold**: as cold as ice, glacial
oven: where you bake pastry or roast meat □ **pretty** *(fam)*: rather
rough: plain, not refined □ **peasants**: simple country people
once in a blue moon: very rarely (when has anyone seen a blue
moon?)
wanders: walks at random, strolls apparently aimlessly
it's no good: it's no use, it's useless, there's no point (trying)
hare = *lièvre* □ **chat**: informal conversation, gossip
now and then: from time to time □ **a bit of money**: some cash
buy him tobacco: purchase tobacco for him □ **gets**: receives
treat him all right: deal kindly with him
like a child: as if he were a child

child. I'm afraid her husband's not very nice to him. He grudges the cost of his keep. I don't believe he's cruel or anything like that, but I think he's a bit sharp with him. He makes him fetch water and clean the cow-shed and that sort of thing."

"It sounds pretty rotten," I said.

"He brought it on himself. After all, he's only got what he deserved."

"I think on the whole we all get what we deserve," I said.
10 "But that doesn't prevent its being rather horrible."

Two or three days later my friend and I were taking a walk. We were strolling along a narrow path through an olive grove.

"There's Wilson," said my friend suddenly. "Don't look, you'll only frighten him. Go straight on."

I walked with my eyes on the path, but out of the corners of them I saw a man hiding behind an olive tree. He did not move as we approached, but I felt that he was watching us. As soon as we had passed I heard a scamper. Wilson, like
20 a hunted animal, had made for safety. That was the last I ever saw of him.

He died last year. He had endured that life for six years. He was found one morning on the mountainside lying quite peacefully as though he had died in his sleep. From where he lay he had been able to see those two great rocks called the Faraglioni which stand out of the sea. It was full moon and he must have gone to see them by moonlight. Perhaps he died of the beauty of that sight.

I'm afraid : I'm sorry to say, I regret to say □ **he grudges** : he regrets; is unwilling to pay □ **the cost of his keep** : what it costs to keep him
a bit sharp : rather brusque, rough
makes him fetch : forces him to bring, go for □ **cow-shed** = *étable*

pretty rotten : rather awful/ dreadful
he brought it on himself : he was responsible for it; it was his own fault; he has only himself to blame for it □ **deserved** : merited
on the whole : generally speaking, as a (general) rule, all in all
prevent its being : prevent it from being, stop it(s) being

strolling : walking leisurely □ **narrow** ≠ wide, broad □ **path** : alley
olive grove : place where olive trees grow
there's Wilson : there he is (note the order of words)
frighten him : scare him (away) □ **go straight on** : don't turn round
out of the corners of them : glancing without appearing to look
hiding : concealing himself, in hiding
felt *(feel, felt, felt)* : had the feeling, the impression □ **watching us** : spying on us □ **scamper** : sound of someone in a hurry
hunted : that people were trying to kill □ **made for** : rushed towards
□ **that was the last I ever saw of him** : I never saw him again
endured : put up with, stood, borne
mountainside : side of the mountain
as though : as if □ **in his sleep** : while he slept
lay *(lie, lay, lain)* = was lying
stand : rise vertically
must have gone : had very probably (almost certainly) gone
died of the beauty... : the beauty... caused his death

Grammaire au fil des nouvelles

Traduisez les phrases suivantes inspirées du texte (le premier chiffre renvoie à la page, les suivants aux lignes).

J'aimerais qu'il se retourne (commençons par : *I wish...* quel temps du verbe pour indiquer un présent non actualisé ? 70 - 10).

Nous regardions les gens qui se promenaient de long en large (tout est inachevé ici... 70 - 18).

Il portait une chemise bleue en coton et un pantalon gris (one article of clothing can be plural, 72 - 11,12).

Nous avions l'habitude de nous baigner tous les jours (a simple habit, but what is the idiom? 74 - 28).

Ce long discours lui avait donné soif (he was thirsty, but the speech had also made him happy, 84 - 18).

C'était le genre de femme qui ne cessait de se demander ce que les gens penseraient (*always + -ing = emph,* 88 - 5,6).

Cela faisait quinze ans qu'il était sur l'île (88 - 16,17).

Pourquoi ne pas tout abandonner (*why not chuck it all up?* mais commençons par : *what's wrong...* 88 - 22) **?**

La banque ne donnait la retraite qu'au bout de trente années de services (pension you off? not till after... 90 - 20).

Il me semblait que cela valait la peine de payer le prix pour avoir vingt-cinq années de bonheur (worth how much? worth paying what price? paying for what? 92 - 18).

La chambre était meublée comme une cellule de moine (génitif générique ; cf.: *a banker's dream,* 94 - 19).

Son propriétaire, dont la femme s'appelait Assunta, se contenta de laisser aller les choses pendant plusieurs mois (après *whose* quel article ? *the* ou *Ø*? 100 - 27,29).

Son propriétaire le somma de quitter la maison s'il ne payait pas les arriérés de loyer avant une certaine date (*not + before* ou *not + by*...oui...mais pensons à *unless,* 102 - 4).

Quoique sa situation fût désespérée, il n'en avait pas souffert (commençons par *desperate* plutôt que par *although,* 102 - 12,13).

Wilson avait dû aller voir ces deux grands rochers, qu'on appelle les Faraglioni (une hypothèse... une probabilité, 106 - 27).

The Man with the Scar

Appearances can be deceptive, and a drug dealer may very well dress like a respectable citizen. But a scar is not a disguise you can put on and take off like a suit of clothes. It suggests a world of violence.

Of violence there is plenty in this story, which mingles love, honour, jealousy, politics, banditry, executions and murder...

It was on account of the scar that I first noticed him, for it ran, broad and red, in a great crescent from his temple to his chin. It must have been due to a formidable wound and I wondered whether this had been caused by a sabre or by a fragment of shell. It was unexpected on that round, fat, and good-humoured face. He had small and undistinguished features, and his expression was artless. His face went oddly with his corpulent body. He was a powerful man of more than common height. I never saw him in anything but
10 a very shabby grey suit, a khaki shirt, and a battered sombrero. He was far from clean. He used to come into the Palace Hotel at Guatemala City every day at cocktail time and strolling leisurely round the bar offer lottery tickets for sale. If this was the way he made his living it must have been a poor one for I never saw anyone buy, but now and then I saw him offered a drink. He never refused it. He threaded his way among the tables with a sort of rolling walk as though he were accustomed to traverse long distances on foot, paused at each table, with a little smile mentioned the
20 numbers he had for sale, and then, when no notice was taken of him, with the same smile passed on. I think he was for the most part a trifle the worse for liquor.

I was standing at the bar one evening, my foot on the rail, with an acquaintance —they make a very good dry Martini at the Palace Hotel in Guatemala City— when the man with the scar came up. I shook my head as for the twentieth time since my arrival he held out for my inspection his lottery tickets. But my companion nodded affably.

"*Qué tal, general?* How is life?"
30   "Not so bad. Business is none too good, but it might be worse."

"What will you have, general?"

110

on account of: because of □ **scar** = *cicatrice* □ **noticed**: perceived
ran: went □ **broad** = narrow, thin □ **crescent**: curve □ **temple**:
forehead □ **chin** = *menton* □ **due to**: caused by □ **wound**: cut
received in a fight □ **wondered**: asked myself □ **had been caused
by**: had resulted from □ **shell**: artillery projectile □ **unexpected**:
surprising □ **fat** ≠ thin □ **good-humoured**: good-tempered □
undistinguished: common □ **features**: traits □ **artless**: innocent □
went oddly with: contrasted strangely with □ **body**: figure □ **of
more than common height**: taller than the usual (average) man
shabby: worn ≠ smart □ **suit**: jacket & trousers □ **shirt** = *chemise*
□ **battered**: worn, knocked about □ **far from clean**: very dirty

strolling: walking slowly (like sb who had leisure, spare time □ **for
sale**: to sell *(sold, sold)* □ **living**: enough money to live; cost
(standard) of living □ **it must have been a poor one**: it couldn't have
been a good living □ **him offered...**: sb offer him (a drink)
with a... rolling walk: swinging, swaying his body as he walked
accustomed to traverse: in the habit of crossing

no notice was taken of him: nobody paid any attention to him
passed on: went on his way
for the most part: most of the time, mostly □ **a trifle**: a little □ **the
worse for liquor**: drunk, tipsy
acquaintance: casual friend, not a close friend

shook my head: indicated a negative answer with my head
since my arrival: since I (had) arrived
nodded: here = gestured "Hello". Can also mean "yes".
how is life?: how are you getting on?
none too good: not very good □ **it might be worse**: it could be less
good; I mustn't complain
what... have?: what will you have (to drink)

"A brandy."

He tossed it down and put the glass back on the bar. He nodded to my acquaintance.

"*Gracias. Hasta luego.*"

Then he turned away and offered his tickets to the men who were standing next to us.

"Who is your friend?" I asked. "That's a terrific scar on his face."

"It doesn't add to his beauty, does it? He's an exile from
10 Nicaragua. He's a ruffian of course and a bandit, but not a bad fellow. I give him a few *pesos* now and then. He was a revolutionary general, and if his ammunition hadn't given out he'd have upset the government and been Minister of War now instead of selling lottery tickets in Guatemala. They captured him, along with his staff, such as it was, and tried him by court-martial. Such things are rather summary in these countries, you know, and he was sentenced to be shot at dawn. I guess he knew what was coming to him when he was caught. He spent the night in gaol and he and the
20 others, there were five of them altogether, passed the time playing poker. They used matches for chips. He told me he'd never had such a run of bad luck in his life; they were playing with a short pack, Jacks to open, but he never held a card; he never improved more than half a dozen times in the whole sitting and no sooner did he buy a new stack than he lost it. When day broke and the soldiers came into the cell to fetch them for execution he had lost more matches than a reasonable man could use in a lifetime.

"They were led into the patio of the gaol and placed
30 against a wall, the five of them side by side, with the firing party facing them. There was a pause and our friend asked the officer in charge of them what the devil they were

112

a brandy: a glass of cognac (or any liquor distilled from wine)
tossed it down: swallowed (in one gulp, at one toss)
nodded: here gave a friendly sign of approbation

turned away: turned his back (on us) □ **offered**: proposed
next to us: directly by us; our next-door neighbours
terrific: terrible, awful, dreadful, appalling

add to his beauty: make him (any) more beautiful, handsome
ruffian: scoundrel, rogue, good-for-nothing
fellow: chap; *(Am)* guy □ **now and then**: from time to time
ammunition *(uncountable)* = bullets, grenades, bombs, shells, etc.
given out: been used, finished; come to an end □ **upset**: overthrown
instead of selling: in place of selling, rather than selling
staff: team □ **such as it was**: although it was not a very good one
tried: put him on trial □ **court-martial**: military court
sentenced to be shot: condemned (by law) to face a firing squad
dawn: sunrise, daybreak □ **coming to him**: in store for him
caught *(catch, caught, caught)*: captured □ **gaol**: jail, prison
there were five of them: note the structure; *how many of them were
there in gaol?* □ **matches** = *allumettes* □ **chips** = *jetons*
a run of bad luck: a series of unlucky (lost) games
short pack: fewer than 52 cards □ **Jacks** = *valets* □ **held a card**:
had a good hand of cards □ **improved**: had better luck
no sooner did he buy: *(note inversion)* he no sooner bought □ **stack**:
pile, supply (of matches) □ **Ø day broke**: Ø dawn came
fetch: take them away, collect
reasonable: sensible, prudent, cautious □ **a lifetime**: a whole life
led *(lead, led, led)*: taken, conducted □ **placed**: stood
the five of them: note the structure. See line 20 □ **firing party**: firing
squad who were to shoot them
in charge of: responsible for □ **what the devil**: what the hell

keeping him waiting for. The officer said that the general commanding the government troops wished to attend the execution and they awaited his arrival.

" 'Then I have time to smoke another cigarette,' said our friend. 'He was always unpunctual.'

"But he had barely lit it when the general —it was San Ignacio, by the way: I don't know whether you ever met him— followed by his A.D.C. came into the patio. The usual formalities were performed and San Ignacio asked the
10 condemned men whether there was anything they wished before the execution took place. Four of the five shook their heads, but our friend spoke.

" 'Yes, I should like to say good-bye to my wife.'

" '*Bueno*,' said the general, 'I have no objection to that. Where is she?'

" 'She is waiting at the prison door.'

" 'Then it will not cause a delay of more than five minutes.'

" 'Hardly that, *Señor General*,' said our friend.
20 " 'Have him placed on one side.'

"Two soldiers advanced and between them the condemned rebel walked to the spot indicated. The officer in command of the firing squad on a nod from the general gave an order, there was a ragged report, and the four men fell. They fell strangely, not together, but one after the other, with movements that were almost grotesque, as though they were puppets in a toy theatre. The officer went up to them and into one who was still alive emptied two barrels of his revolver. Our friend finished his cigarette and
30 threw away the stub.

"There was a little stir at the gateway. A woman came into the patio, with quick steps, and then, her hand on her

114

what... keeping him waiting for : why (they were) making him wait
commanding : in command of □ **attend :** be present at
awaited his arrival : waited for him to arrive

always unpunctual : never on time, always behind time (late)
barely... when : hardly, scarcely... when; barely had he lit it when
by the way : incidentally □ **met** *(meet, met, met)* **him :** made his
acquaintance □ **A.D.C. :** aide-de-camp
formalities were performed : ceremonies were gone through
condemned : sentenced to death (N.B. prison or a fine = *sentenced*)
took place : was performed □ **shook... heads :** gave a negative
answer by moving their heads from side to side ≠ *nodded* (their
heads)
I have no objection to that : I don't object to (you doing) that

cause a delay : make us (more than 5 minutes) late; hold the
execution up (by more than 5 minutes)
hardly that : not even as long as that, not even that long
have him placed : give orders for him to be put; let him be put
advanced : stepped forward
spot : place □ **officer in command :** commanding officer
firing squad : firing party □ **nod** ≠ shake of the head cf. line 11
ragged ≠ simultaneous □ **report :** sound of guns firing
fell *(fall, fell, fallen)* **:** dropped together at the same time

puppets : marionnettes □ **toy theatre :** miniature theatre for children
emptied two barrels : fired two shots
threw *(throw, threw, thrown)* **away :** tossed away, cast away
stub : (cigarette or cigar) end; butt
stir : movement, bustle □ **gateway :** opening of the gate. N.B. a *gate*
is outside; a *door(way)* is inside the entrance of a house

heart, stopped suddenly. She gave a cry and with outstretched arms ran forward.

"'*Caramba*,' said the general.

"She was in black, with a veil over her hair, and her face was dead white. She was hardly more than a girl, a slim creature, with little regular features and enormous eyes. But they were distraught with anguish. Her loveliness was such that as she ran, her mouth slightly open and the agony of her face beautiful, a gasp of surprise was wrung from those
10 indifferent soldiers who looked at her.

"The rebel advanced a step or two to meet her. She flung herself into his arms and with a hoarse cry of passion: *alma de mi corazón*, soul of my heart, he pressed his lips to hers. And at the same moment he drew a knife from his ragged shirt —I haven't a notion how he managed to retain possession of it— and stabbed her in the neck. The blood spurted from the cut vein and dyed his shirt. Then he flung his arms round her and once more pressed his lips to hers.

"It happened so quickly that many did not know what
20 had occurred, but from the others burst a cry of horror; they sprang forward and seized him. They loosened his grasp and the girl would have fallen if the A.D.C. had not caught her. She was unconscious. They laid her on the ground and with dismay on their faces stood round watching her. The rebel knew where he was striking and it was impossible to staunch the blood. In a moment the A.D.C. who had been kneeling by her side rose.

"'She's dead,' he whispered.

"The rebel crossed himself.

30 "'Why did you do it?' asked the general.

"'I loved her.'

"A sort of sigh passed through those men crowded

116

heart = *cœur* □ **gave a cry**: uttered an involuntary shout
outstretched: wide apart

hair *(uncountable)* = *cheveu(x)*
dead white: pure white □ **hardly more**: little more □ **slim**: slender
features: facial traits
distraught with anguish: distracted with anguish, with grief
slightly: a little □ **agony**: anguish, grief, pain
gasp: sudden intake of breath □ **wrung** *(wring, wrung, wrung)*:
torn, forced, extracted
advanced a step or two: stepped forward slightly □ **flung** *(fling,
flung, flung)*: threw, cast □ **hoarse**: not clear; muffled, throaty

drew *(draw, drew, drawn)*: pulled out □ **knife** = *couteau* □ **ragged**:
torn, tattered □ **shirt** = *chemise* □ **retain**: keep
stabbed: struck (with the point of a knife) □ **blood** = *sang*
spurted: flowed out (under pressure), gushed □ **dyed**: coloured
once more: again, one more time

occurred: taken place □ **burst**: came suddenly and spontaneously
sprang *(spring, sprang, sprung)*: jumped □ **loosened his grasp**: made
him let go (his grip)
was unconscious: had lost consciousness □ **laid**: placed (flat)
dismay: consternation; they were dismayed □ **stood round**:
surrounded (her) □ **striking**: hitting, stabbing
staunch the blood: stop the blood flowing
kneeling: on his knees □ **by her side**: beside her □ **rose**: stood up

crossed himself: made the sign of the cross

sigh: heavy breath of sadness; they sighed, heaved a sigh

117

together and they looked with strange faces at the murderer. The general stared at him for a while in silence.

" 'It was a noble gesture,' he said at last. 'I cannot execute this man. Take my car and have him led to the frontier. *Señor*, I offer you the homage which is due from one brave man to another.'

"A murmur of approbation broke from those who listened. The A.D.C. tapped the rebel on the shoulder, and between the two soldiers without a word he marched to the

10 waiting car."

My friend stopped and for a little I was silent. I must explain that he was a Guatemalecan and spoke to me in Spanish. I have translated what he told me as well as I could, but I have made no attempt to tone down his rather high-flown language. To tell the truth I think it suits the story.

"But how then did he get the scar?" I asked at length.

"Oh, that was due to a bottle that burst when I was opening it. A bottle of ginger ale."

"I never liked it," said I.

faces: an (odd) expression on their faces □ **murderer**: assassin
stared at him: looked fixedly at him □ **for a while**: for some time

have him led: let him be led, taken, accompanied □ **frontier**: border
offer you the homage: pay you the homage

murmur of approbation: approving murmur □ **broke**: rose, was
torn □ **tapped**: touched (to attract his attention) □ **shoulder** =
épaule □ **marched**: walked in military fashion
waiting: which was waiting (for him to arrive)
was silent: did not speak; waited before speaking again

as well as I could: as best I could
made no attempt: not attempted, not tried □ **tone down**: attenuate
high-flown: grandiloquent, flamboyant □ **suits**: is appropriate
for □ **scar**: visible sign of a wound □ **at length**: after a while
burst *(burst, burst, burst)*: exploded, blew up
ginger ale = ginger beer (gassy non-alcoholic drink)
I never liked it: it's something I never liked

Grammaire au fil des nouvelles

Traduisez les phrases suivantes inspirées du texte (le premier chiffre renvoie à la page, les suivants aux lignes).

La cicatrice devait certainement provenir d'une terrible blessure (quasi-certitude, donc quel auxiliaire modal? 110 - 3).

Je me demandais si cette cicatrice avait été causée par un coup de sabre ou par un éclat d'obus (sabre slash? fragment of shell? I wonder... 110 - 4,5).

Je ne lui ai jamais vu porter autre chose qu'un costume gris très élimé (he was always in grey... nothing but grey, 110 - 9).

Il était loin d'être propre (a-t-on besoin de *be*? 110 - 11).

C'était ainsi qu'il gagnait sa vie (the way... 110 - 14).

Il avançait à travers les tables... comme s'il était habitué à couvrir de grandes distances à pied (as if/though he were/was... 110 - 16).

Je me tenais devant le bar... lorsque l'homme à la cicatrice s'avança (formes verbales : prétérit simple ou progressif? 110 - 25).

S'il n'avait pas été à court de munitions il aurait renversé le gouvernement (*his ammunition had in fact given out,* mais ici tout est au conditionnel, 112 - 12,13).

Ils étaient 5 (*they were 5* = ils avaient 5 ans! 112 - 20).

Ils passaient le temps à jouer au poker (you play the piano, the guitar etc. but you play Ø golf, tennis etc. 112 - 20).

Il n'avait pas plus tôt acheté un nouveau paquet qu'il le perdait (remember : *no sooner...than; hardly/scarcely...when/ before...* et après une locution négative ou restrictive en tête de phrase : *inversion!* 112 - 25).

Faites mettre cet homme sur le côté (phrase au sens passif, donc le verbe causatif ici = *make? have?* 114 - 20).

Un instant après, l'A.D.C., qui était agenouillé auprès d'elle, se leva (positions du corps = *-ed* ou *-ing?* 116 - 26).

Faites-le conduire à la frontière (*v. causatif* encore, 118 - 4).

J'ai traduit ce qu'il me disait de mon mieux (idée de possibilité = *superlatif? comparatif d'égalité?* 118 - 13).

Gigolo and Gigolette

We are on the French Riviera — the Côte d'Azur — among the fashionable cosmopolitan society that crowd the casinos and night clubs during the season. The latest craze is a young girl who dives from a high platform into a shallow tank of water.

Somerset Maugham gives us first a ring-side seat, where we can see and hear the wealthy commenting on the act. We learn about their motivations in coming regularly night after night to the same club to eat much the same food and see the identical high dive. One of the attractions of the show is certainly the thrill of the risk involved...

Then we move behind the scenes, into the wings and right into the artist's dressing-room, where the performer can take off the mask she wears in public, along with the glittering tinsel and bright lights of the show business. We learn how she and her male partner fell in love with each other, how they lived before and during the dark years of the Depression. And most importantly, we find out how they regard their public and how they think their public regards them. A love-hate relationship...

The bar was crowded. Sandy Westcott had had a couple of cocktails and he was beginning to feel hungry. He looked at his watch. He had been asked to dinner at half past nine and it was nearly ten. Eva Barrett was always late and he would be lucky if he got anything to eat by ten-thirty. He turned to the barman to order another cocktail and caught sight of a man who at that moment came up to the bar.

"Hullo, Cotman," he said. "Have a drink?"

"I don't mind if I do, sir."

10   Cotman was a nice-looking fellow, of thirty perhaps, short, but with so good a figure that he did not look it, very smartly dressed in a double-breasted dinner jacket, a little too much waisted, and a butterfly tie a good deal too large. He had a thick mat of black, wavy hair, very sleek and shiny, brushed straight back from his forehead, and large flashing eyes. He spoke with great refinement, but with a Cockney accent.

"How's Stella?" asked Sandy.

"Oh, she's all right. Likes to have a lay-down before the 20 show, you know. Steadies the old nerves, she says."

"I wouldn't do that stunt of hers for a thousand pounds."

"I don't suppose you would. No one can do it but her, not from that height, I mean, and only five foot of water."

"It's the most sick-making thing I've ever seen."

Cotman gave a little laugh. He took this as a compliment. Stella was his wife. Of course she did the trick and took the risk, but it was he who had thought of the flames, and it was the flames that had taken the public fancy and made the 30 turn the huge success it was. Stella dived into a tank from the top of a ladder sixty feet high, and as he said, there were only five feet of water in the tank. Just before she dived

crowded : there was a large crowd in the bar □ **a couple** : two or three □ **feel** *(felt, felt)* **hungry** : feel like having a meal

watch : instrument for telling the time □ **asked** : invited

always late : never on time

lucky : in luck; it would be a piece of luck □ **by** : before

cocktail : what you drink at a cocktail party □ **caught sight** : got a glimpse □ **at that moment** : just then

have a drink? : (will you) have something to drink?

I don't mind if I do : I don't mind having one; I have no objection to having one (= I would like one) □ **nice-looking** : handsome, good-looking □ **so good a figure** : such a good body, built

smartly : elegantly □ **double-breasted** = *croisé* □ **dinner jacket** : black suit for evening wear; *(Am)* tuxedo □ **waisted** : close-fitting □ **butterfly tie** = *nœud papillon* □ **mat** : mass □ **wavy** ≠ straight □ **sleek** : unnaturally brilliant □ **shiny** ≠ dull □ **forehead** : the front of his head □ **flashing** : shining like diamonds or lightning

Cockney : working- class London

how's Stella : how is Stella keeping?

likes to have a lay-down *(fam)* : (she) like to lie down in bed

steadies : (it) stabilises, calms down □ **the old nerves** *(fam)* = her nerves □ **that stunt of hers** *(emph)* = her number, act, turn

you would : you would (like to do it)

five foot = 1 metre 53. Note the singular often used instead of *feet* as a unit of measure □ **sick-making** : frightening; it makes me feel sick □ **took** : accepted, interpreted

wife ≠ husband □ **trick** : act, turn, stunt, number

it was he who *(emph)* : he was the one who

taken the public fancy : captured the imagination of the public

turn : act □ **huge** : enormous □ **dived** : plunged □ **tank** : receptacle for holding liquids *e.g.* petrol tank; cf. oil tanker □ **ladder** = *échelle* □ **sixty feet high** = over 18 metres high (cf. line 24)

they poured enough petrol on to cover the surface and he set it alight; the flames soared up and she dived straight into them.

"Paco Espinel tells me it's the biggest draw the Casino has ever had," said Sandy.

"I know. He told me they'd served as many dinners in July as they generally do in August. And that's you, he says to me."

"Well, I hope you're making a packet."

10 "Well, I can't exactly say that. You see, we've got our contract and naturally we didn't know it was going to be a riot, but Mr. Espinel's talking of booking us for next month, and I don't mind telling you he's not going to get us on the same terms or anything like it. Why, I had a letter from an agent only this morning saying they wanted us to go to Deauville."

"Here are my people," said Sandy.

He nodded to Cotman and left him. Eva Barrett sailed in with the rest of her guests. She had gathered them 20 together downstairs. It was a party of eight.

"I knew we should find you here, Sandy," she said. "I'm not late, am I?"

"Only half an hour."

"Ask them what cocktails they want and then we'll dine."

While they were standing at the bar, emptying now, for nearly everyone had gone down to the terrace for dinner, Paco Espinel passed through and stopped to shake hands with Eva Barrett. Paco Espinel was a young man who had 30 run through his money and now made his living by arranging the turns with which the Casino sought to attract visitors. It was his duty to be civil to the rich and great.

petrol: refined product from oil wells
set *(set, set, set)* **it alight**: set fire to it □ **soared up**: rose quickly in huge flames
draw: attraction; cf. verb: draw *(drew, drawn)* = attract

told me: said to me □ **they'd**: they had (served)
generally: usually; as a general rule □ **that's you**: that's (because of) you
making a packet *(slang)*: making a lot of money, a fortune

naturally: of course
a riot: here = a great success □ **booking**: reserving
I don't mind telling you *(idiom)* = I'm telling you emphatically
terms: conditions □ **or anything like it**: or very similar □ **why** *(excl)*: for instance; after all, etc. □ **wanted us to go**: were anxious for us to go (N.B. *infinitive clause*)
my people: the people I am supposed to meet; my friends
nodded: moved his head to say goodbye □ **sailed in**: entered majestically □ **gathered**: assembled
it was a party of eight: there were eight of them
I'm not late, am I? ≠ I'm late, aren't I? (note the form of the question tags: *am I* but *aren't I*)

what cocktails they want: what kind of cocktails they want
dine: have dinner
emptying now: (which was) emptying ≠ filling now
for dinner: note the zero article before the principal meals
passed through: crossed the room □ **shake** *(shook, shaken)* **hands with her**: shake her hand, shake her by the hand
run through: spent, squandered □ **made his living**: earned his living (N.B. *cost of living* i.e. economic, but *quality of life*) □ **sought** *(lit)*: tried □ **duty**: obligation □ **civil**: courteous, polite

Mrs. Chaloner Barrett was an American widow of vast wealth; she not only entertained expensively, but also gambled. And after all, the dinners and suppers and the two cabaret shows that accompanied them were only provided to induce people to lose their money at the tables.

"Got a good table for me, Paco?" said Eva Barrett.

"The best." His eyes, fine, dark Argentine eyes, expressed his admiration of Mrs. Barrett's opulent, ageing charms. This also was business. "You've seen Stella?"

10   "Of course. Three times. It's the most terrifying thing I've ever seen."

"Sandy comes every night."

"I want to be in at the death. She's bound to kill herself one of these nights and I don't want to miss that if I can help it."

Paco laughed.

"She's been such a success, we're going to keep her on another month. All I ask is that she shouldn't kill herself till the end of August. After that she can do as she likes."

20   "Oh, God, have I got to go on eating trout and roast chicken every night till the end of August?" cried Sandy.

"You brute, Sandy," said Eva Barrett. "Come on, let's go in to dinner. I'm starving."

Paco Espinel asked the barman if he'd seen Cotman. The barman said he'd had a drink with Mr. Westcott.

"Oh, well, if he comes in here again, tell him I want a word with him."

Mrs. Barrett paused at the top of the steps that led down to the terrace long enough for the press representative, a
30 little haggard woman with an untidy head, to come up with her note-book. Sandy whispered the names of the guests. It was a representative Riviera party. There was an English

126

widow: whose husband was dead □ **of vast wealth**: enormously wealthy, rich, affluent □ **entertained expensively**: gave expensive parties □ **gambled**: played for money (especially at games of chance) □ **shows**: entertainments □ **provided**: given

induce: tempt □ **lose** *(lost, lost)* ≠ win □ **tables**: roulette, etc.

got: (have you) got

fine: beautiful, handsome

opulent: plump □ **ageing**: fading

business *(U)*: business is business

thing I've ever seen: thing (that) I've seen in my life

in at the death *(hunting idiom)* = in at the kill (when the fox is trapped) □ **she's bound to kill herself**: she's certain, sure to be killed; she can't help killing herself

laughed: gave a laugh; burst out laughing

such a success: so successful □ **keep her on** ≠ send her away

shouldn't kill herself: note *should* after a verb of coercion; *e.g.* he insisted that she *shouldn't* leave

have I got to go on eating: must I keep eating □ **trout** = *truite* (N.B. no -*s* in plural, like other nouns referring to game)

come on *(excl):* here = hurry up

starving: dying of hunger; ravenous

if he'd seen: whether he had seen

he'd had a drink: N.B. the verb *have* with food and drink

I want a word with him: I want (to have) a word with him, to say a few words to him

steps: the flight of steps (N.B. steps outside = stairs inside)

long enough: a long enough period of time □ **representative**: person representing (the press) □ **untidy** ≠ tidy, neat □ **head**: here = hair i.e. head of hair □ **whispered**: said in a low voice, in an undertone

representative: typical, characteristic

127

Lord and his Lady, long and lean both of them, who were prepared to dine with anyone who would give them a free meal. They were certain to be as tight as drums before midnight. There was a gaunt Scotch woman, with a face like a Peruvian mask that has been battered by the storms of ten centuries, and her English husband. Though a broker by profession, he was bluff, military, and hearty. He gave you an impression of such integrity that you were almost more sorry for him than for yourself when the good thing he had 10 put you on to as a special favour turned out to be a dud. There was an Italian countess who was neither Italian nor a countess, but played a beautiful game of bridge, and there was a Russian prince who was ready to make Mrs. Barrett a princess and in the meantime sold champagne, motor-cars, and Old Masters on commission. A dance was in progress, and Mrs. Barrett, waiting for it to end, surveyed with a look which her short upper lip made scornful the serried throng on the dance floor. It was a gala night and the dining tables were crowded together. Beyond the terrace 20 the sea was calm and silent. The music stopped and the head waiter, affably smiling, came up to guide her to her table. She swept down the steps with majestic gait.

"We shall have quite a good view of the dive," she said as she sat down.

"I like to be next door to the tank," said Sandy, "so that I can see her face."

"Is she pretty?" asked the Countess.

"It's not that. It's the expression of her eyes. She's scared to death every time she does it."

30   "Oh, I don't believe that," said the City gentleman, Colonel Goodhart by name, though no one had ever

lean: thin

prepared: ready, willing □ **dine**: have dinner □ **a free meal**: a meal for nothing □ **tight as drums**: 1) tense as drums (= *tambours*) 2) here = *fig* = as drunk as lords □ **gaunt**: emaciated

battered: beaten repeatedly □ **storms** *(fig)*: vicissitudes

broker: investor on the Stock Exchange

bluff: direct and jovial □ **hearty**: vigorously friendly

were... sorry for him: pitied him

good thing he had put you on to: good investment he had indicated

turned out to be: proved to be; showed itself finally to be □ **dud**: illusion; false hope

ready: prepared, willing □ **make... princess**: transform... into a princess □ **in the meantime**: while waiting; meanwhile

on commission: for a percentage; on a percentage basis

waiting for it to end: waiting until it ended

short ≠ long □ **upper** ≠ lower □ **lip** = *lèvre* □ **made scornful**: rendered contemptuous ≠ admiring □ **serried throng**: dense crowd

crowded together: very close ≠ far apart □ **beyond**: outside

head waiter: person in charge of those who served at table

swept down: descended majestically □ **steps**: flight of steps □ **gait**: carriage; manner of walking □ **quite a good view**: a fairly good sight (N.B. order of words)

next door: close by, right beside; as close as can be □ **so that I can see**: (for me) to be able to see

pretty: good-looking ≠ plain, ugly

it's not that: that's not the point, not what I mean □ **scared to death**: as frightened as can be □ **every time she does it**: each time (that) she dives □ **City**: business centre of London

Colonel... by name: called... Colonel

discovered how he came by the title. "I mean, the whole bally stunt's only a trick. There's no danger really, I mean."

"You don't know what you're talking about. Diving from that height in as little water as that, she's got to turn like a flash the moment she touches the water. And if she doesn't do it right she's bound to bash her head against the bottom and break her back."

"That's just what I'm telling you, old boy," said the Colonel, "it's a trick. I mean, there's no argument."

10 "If there's no danger there's nothing to it, anyway," said Eva Barrett. "It's over in a minute. Unless she's risking her life it's the biggest fraud of modern times. Don't say we've come to see this over and over again and it's only a fake."

"Pretty well everything is. You can take my word for that."

"Well, you ought to know," said Sandy.

If it occurred to the Colonel that this might be a nasty dig he admirably concealed it. He laughed.

"I don't mind saying I know a thing or two," he admitted.
20 "I mean, I've got my eyes peeled all right. You can't put much over on me."

The tank was on the far left of the terrace, and behind it, supported by stays, was an immensely tall ladder at the top of which was a tiny platform. After two or three dances more, when Eva Barrett's party were eating asparagus, the music stopped and the lights were lowered. A spot was turned on the tank. Cotman was visible in the brilliance. He ascended half a dozen steps so that he was on a level with the top of the tank.

30 "Ladies and gentlemen," he cried out, in a loud clear voice, "you are now going to see the most marvellous feat of the century. Madam Stella, the greatest diver in the world,

discovered : found out □ **came by** : acquired □ **I mean** : it's my opinion □ **stunt** : turn, act □ **trick** : deception, fake, fraud

know what you're talking about : know the subject; what it implies

as little water as that : so little water □ **like a flash** : like lightning

the moment : as soon as □ **doesn't do it right** : makes a mistake

bound : certain, sure □ **bash** *(fam)* : hit, knock, strike

back : spinal column

old boy *(fam)* : my friend

there's no argument : there's no doubt; it's unquestionable

there's nothing to it : it's very easy

over : finished, ended □ **unless she's risking** : if she isn't risking

fraud : deception, cheat, fake

over and over again : repeatedly : time and time again □ **fake** : trick, fraud □ **pretty well** : almost □ **you can take my word for that** : you can believe me (on that score)

you ought to know : you should know; you are the person to know

it occurred to the Colonel : the Colonel had the idea □ **nasty** : bad malicious □ **dig** : offensive remark □ **concealed** : disguised

I don't mind saying : I'm willing to say □ **admitted** : confessed

I've got my eyes peeled *(fig)* : I'm clear-sighted □ **put much over on me** : deceive, cheat me easily

on the far left : to the extreme left (hand side)

supported : held □ **stays** : supporting cables □ **ladder** = *échelle*

tiny : very small □ **two or three dances more** : another two or three dances □ **asparagus** *(sing & plur)* = *asperge(s)*

lowered : diminished □ **spot** : spot light

turned : directed

on a level with : at the same height as

top : summit

cried out : shouted □ **loud** ≠ soft, low

feat : exploit, accomplishment, achievement

greatest diver : diving champion

is about to dive from a height of sixty feet into a lake of flames five foot deep. This is a feat that has never been performed before, and Madam Stella is prepared to give one hundred pounds to anyone who will attempt it. Ladies and gentlemen, I have the honour to present Madam Stella."

A little figure appeared at the top of the steps that led on to the terrace, ran quickly up to the tank, and bowed to the applauding audience. She wore a man's silk dressing-gown and on her head a bathing-cap. Her thin face was made up
10 as if for the stage. The Italian countess looked at her through her *face-à-main*.

"Not pretty," she said.

"Good figure," said Eva Barrett. "You'll see."

Stella slipped out of her dressing-gown and gave it to Cotman. He went down the steps. She stood for a moment and looked at the crowd. They were in darkness and she could only see vague white faces and white shirt-fronts. She was small, beautifully made, with legs long for her body and slim hips. Her bathing costume was very scanty.

20 "You're quite right about the figure, Eva," said the Colonel. "Bit undeveloped, of course, but I know you girls think that's quite the thing."

Stella began to climb the ladder and the spot-light followed her. It seemed an incredible height. An attendant poured petrol on the surface of the water. Cotman was handed a flaming torch. He watched Stella reach the top of the ladder and settle herself on the platform.

"Ready?" he cried.

"Yes."

30 "Go," he shouted.

And as he shouted he seemed to plunge the burning torch into the water. The flames sprang up, leaping high, and

132

about to dive: on the point of plunging □ **feet** *(plur of foot)*: approximately 30 cm □ **five foot deep**: with a depth of five feet (= 1 ½ metres); N.B. certain measures often keep the *sing* form; cf. 12 stone(s), pound(s) in weight; 5 inch(es) thick □ **attempt it**: try (to perform) it

figure: form, shape □ **led** *(lead, led, led)* **on to**: gave on to

bowed: bent her body to acknowledge the applause

applauding: clapping □ **silk** = *soie* □ **dressing-gown**: *(Am)* bathrobe □ **bathing cap**: to keep the hair dry □ **made up**: with cosmetics, make-up □ **stage**: theatre

not pretty: (she's) not good-looking, attractive

figure: body, shape

slipped out of: took off with a quick, supple movement

went down: descended □ **stood** *(stand, stood, stood)*: remained

white = *blanc* □ **shirt-fronts**: the front part of the shirts (= *chemises)* □ **legs** = *jambes* □ **body**: figure

slim: attractively slender; N.B. thin = *pej*

quite right about...: what you said about the figure was perfectly correct □ **bit**: (a) bit; slightly; rather

quite the thing: absolutely the right thing to be; the fashion

climb the ladder: mount the ladder (= *échelle)*

attendant: help

poured petrol: emptied a can of petrol (= *essence)* □ **was handed**: (Cotman) was given (a torch); (a torch) was handed to him

settle herself: get ready; concentrate for the dive

ready?: (are you) ready?

plunge: thrust, push

sprang *(spring, sprang, sprung)*: jumped, leaped

really terrifying to look at. At the same moment Stella
dived. She came down like a streak of lightning and plunged
through the flames, which subsided a moment after she had
reached the water. A second later she was at the surface and
jumped out to a roar, a storm of applause. Cotman
wrapped the dressing-gown round her. She bowed and
bowed. The applause went on. Music struck up. With a final
wave of the hand she ran down the steps and between the
tables to the door. The lights went up and the waiters
10 hurried along with their neglected service.

Sandy Westcott gave a sigh. He did not know whether he
was disappointed or relieved.

"Top hole," said the English peer.

"It's a bally fake," said the Colonel, with his British
pertinacity. "I bet you anything you like."

"It's over so quickly," said her English ladyship. "I mean,
you don't get your money's worth really."

Anyhow it wasn't her money. That it never was. The
Italian countess leaned forward. She spoke fluent English,
20 but with a strong accent.

"Eva, my darling, who are those extraordinary people at
the table near the door under the balcony?"

"Packet of fun, aren't they?" said Sandy. "I simply
haven't been able to take my eyes off them."

Eva Barrett glanced at the table the Countess indicated,
and the Prince, who sat with his back to it, turned round
to look.

"They can't be true," cried Eva. "I must ask Angelo who
they are."

30 Mrs. Barrett was the sort of woman who knew the head
waiters of all the principal restaurants in Europe by their

134

terrifying to look at: (it was) a terrifying sight

streak: violent flash □ **lightning** *(U) = éclair(s)*

subsided: gradually went out; died down

later ≠ sooner; earlier

roar: loud shout □ **a storm of applause** *(U)*: a frenzied outburst of clapping □ **wrapped**: folded; enveloped (her in the dressing gown)

bowed and bowed: kept bowing time after time □ **struck** *(strike, struck, struck)* **up**: started, began (playing)

went up: became bright again (after having been dimmed)

hurried... service: became active again waiting on the customers

gave a sigh: breathed out (with emotion)

disappointed or relieved: a disappointment or a relief

top hole *(old-fashioned sl)*: excellent; *(modern)* it's the tops

bally *(old-fashioned sl)*: bloody, damn(ed) □ **fake**: trick; cheat

bet: risk money on one's opinion

over: finished □ **her ladyship**: cf. Her Majesty; his lordship

get your money's worth *(idiom)*: get value for your money

anyhow: in any case

leaned forward ≠ bent back(wards) □ **she spoke fluent English**: she spoke English fluently; her English was fluent □ **strong**: marked, pronounced

packet of fun *(slang)*: funny, strange, bizarre

take my eyes off them: stop looking at them

glanced: cast a glance, a quick look

they can't be true: they must be false (i.e. great probability) □ **I must ask**: I mustn't forget to ask (i.e. determination)

sort of woman: kind of woman □ **head waiters**: principal waiters

principal restaurants: top restaurants

first names. She told the waiter who was at that moment filling her glass to send Angelo to her.

It was certainly an odd pair. They were sitting by themselves at a small table. They were very old. The man was big and stout, with a mass of white hair, great bushy white eyebrows, and an enormous white moustache. He looked like the late King Humbert of Italy, but much more like a king. He sat bolt upright. He wore full evening dress, with a white tie and a collar that has been out of fashion
10 for hard on thirty years. His companion was a little old lady in a black satin ball dress, cut very low, and tight at the waist. Round her neck were several chains of coloured beads. She wore what was obviously a wig, and a very ill-fitting one at that; it was very elaborate, all curls and sausages, and raven black. She was outrageously made-up, bright blue under the eyes and on the eyelids, the eyebrows heavily black, a great patch of very pink rouge on each cheek, and the lips a livid scarlet. The skin hung loosely on her face in deep wrinkles. She had large bold eyes and they
20 darted eagerly from table to table. She was taking everything in, and every other minute called the old man's attention to someone or other. The appearance of the couple was so fantastic in that fashionable crowd, the men in dinner jackets, the women in thin, pale-coloured frocks, that many eyes were turned on them. The staring did not seem to incommode the old lady. When she felt certain persons were looking at her she raised her eyebrows archly, smiled and rolled her eyes. She seemed on the point of acknowledging applause.
30   Angelo hurried up to the good customer that Eva Barrett was.

"You wished to see me, my lady?"

knew... by their first names: called them *by* their Christian names

odd pair: strange couple □ **by themselves**: all alone; on their own

stout: corpulent □ **hair**: N.B. *uncountable* — unless each hair is
seen separately! □ **bushy**: hirsute □ **eyebrows** = *sourcils*
the late King: the king who had died □ **much more**: far more; even
more □ **bolt upright**: absolutely straight □ **full evening dress**: the
most formal of evening wear □ **tie** = *cravate*
hard on: nearly, almost □ **companion**: person who accompanied
him □ **a... dress**: distinguish *dress (U)* for either sex *(see 1. 8)* and
a dress — for women only □ **tight** ≠ loose □ **waist** = *taille* □ **neck**
= *cou* □ **beads**: imitation or real pearls or stones □ **obviously**:
evidently □ **a wig**: Ø false hair □ **ill-fitting**: not the right size □ **at
that**: into the bargain □ **raven black**: pure black, jet black
bright: vivid □ **eyelids** = *paupières*
patch: contrasting zone □ **pink**: rose-coloured
lips = *lèvres* □ **scarlet**: red □ **skin** = *peau* □ **hung loosely**: was no
longer firm □ **wrinkles**: folds, loose skin □ **bold**: audacious
darted: moved like arrows □ **eagerly**: with interest, enthusiasm □
taking everything in: absorbing every detail □ **every other minute**:
every couple of minutes □ **someone or other**: first one person, then
another
dinner jackets: *(Am)* tuxedo ≠ full evening dress □ **frocks**: light
dresses □ **the staring**: the fact that people were staring, looking
curiously
raised: lifted □ **archly**: coquettishly

acknowledging applause: thanking the audience for applauding
customer: client, patron

my lady: your ladyship; cf. Your Majesty

"Oh, Angelo, we're simply dying to know who those absolutely marvellous people are at the next table to the door."

Angelo gave a look and then assumed a deprecating air. The expression of his face, the movement of his shoulders, the turn of his spine, the gesture of his hands, probably even the twiddle of his toes, all indicated a half-humorous apology.

"You must overlook them, my lady." He knew of course
10 that Mrs. Barrett had no right to be thus addressed, just as he knew that the Italian countess was neither Italian nor a countess and that the English lord never paid for a drink if anyone else would pay for it, but he also knew that to be thus addressed did not displease her. "They begged me to give them a table because they wanted to see Madam Stella do her dive. They were in the profession themselves once. I know they're not the sort of people one expects to see dining here, but they made such a point of it I simply hadn't the heart to refuse."

20 "But I think they're a perfect scream. I adore them."

"I've known them for many years. The man indeed is a compatriot of mine." The head waiter gave a condescending little laugh. "I told them I'd give them a table on the condition that they didn't dance. I wasn't taking any risks, my lady."

"Oh, but I should have loved to see them dance."

"One has to draw the line somewhere, my lady," said Angelo gravely.

He smiled, bowed again and withdrew.

30 "Look," cried Sandy, "they're going."

The funny old couple were paying their bill. The old man got up and put round his wife's neck a large white, but not

138

we're dying to know: we'd so much like to know
marvellous: wonderful □ **next table to the door**: the table next to the door
deprecating air: disapproving manner; air of disapproval
shoulders = *épaules*
spine: back, spinal column
twiddle: rapid movement back and forward □ **toes** = *orteils*

overlook ≠ pay attention □ **my lady**: your ladyship
had no right: was not entitled □ **thus addressed**: given this title

paid for a drink: note *for*, which indicates an exchange. You give money *in exchange for* a drink
begged me: asked me as a special favour
see... do: see... doing (structure with infinitive *or* gerundive)
once: at one time in the past
expects to see: thinks one will probably find
made such a point of it: insisted so much on it □ **hadn't the heart to refuse**: hadn't the courage to say no; could not resist
a... scream *(fam)*: very amusing; great fun
I've known them for many years: it's many years (now) since I first met them □ **a compatriot of mine**: one of my compatriots
on (the) condition they didn't dance: provided, as long as they didn't dance (note the preterit tense) □ **taking any risks**: running any risks

I should have loved to see them dance: I wish I could have seen them dance □ **draw** *(drew, drawn)* **the line**: make a limit

withdrew *(withdraw, withdrew, withdrawn)*: went away
they're going: they're about to leave
paying their bill: cf. paid for a drink, line 12
put round: wrapped round

139

too clean, feather boa. She rose. He gave her his arm, holding himself very erect, and she, small in comparison, tripped out beside him. Her black satin dress had a long train, and Eva Barrett (who was well over fifty) screamed with joy.

"Look, I remember my mother wearing a dress like that when I was in the schoolroom."

The comic pair walked, still arm in arm, through the spacious rooms of the Casino till they came to the door. The
10 old man addressed a commissionaire.

"Be so good as to direct me to the artistes' dressing-rooms. We wish to pay our respects to Madam Stella."

The commissionaire gave them a look and summed them up. They were not people with whom it was necessary to be very polite.

"You won't find her there."

"She has not gone? I thought she gave a second performance at two?"

"That's true. They might be in the bar."
20   "It won't 'urt us just to go an' 'ave a look, Carlo," said the old lady.

"Right-o, my love," he answered with a great roll of the R.

They walked slowly up the great stairs and entered the bar. It was empty but for the deputy-barman and a couple sitting in two arm-chairs in the corner. The old lady released her husband's arm and tripped up with outstretched hands.

"'Ow are you, dear? I felt I just 'ad to come and
30 congratulate you, bein' English same as you are. And in the profession meself. It's a grand turn, my dear, it deserves to

140

feather boa : boa made of birds' feathers □ **rose** *(rise, rose, risen)* : stood up □ **erect** : straight, upright □ **in comparison** : compared with him □ **tripped out** : walked out, with small, quick steps **well over fifty** : much older than □ **screamed** : shouted

I remember my mother wearing : I recall (the time when) my mother (was) wearing □ **in the schoolroom** : at school
arm in arm *(idiom)* : cf. hand in hand, shoulder to shoulder, etc.

addressed : spoke to □ **commissionaire** : attendant at the door
be so good as to direct me *(fml)* : be good enough to show me the way; please direct me □ **dressing-rooms** : where the artistes dress and make up before the performance □ **summed them up** : measured them up, weighed them up, sized them up

she has not gone? : she hasn't gone, has she? □ **I thought she gave** : I was under the impression she normally gave, was to give
they might be at the bar : it's just a possibility
'urt us = hurt us (imitation of Cockney speech, where the H's are not always pronounced)
right-o *(fam)* : very good □ **a great roll of the R.** : rolling the R (of the word *right-o*) with great vigour
entered the bar : went into the bar; made their entry into it
empty ≠ full □ **but for** : except for, with the exception of
released : let go, stopped holding
tripped : approached with quick, short steps □ **with outstretched hands** : holding out her hands (in greeting)
'ow are you, dear? how do feel, my dear? □ **I just 'ad to come** : I simply couldn't help coming □ **same as you are** *(fam)* : as you are; like you □ **meself** *(fam)* = myself □ **turn** : number

141

be a success." She turned to Cotman. "And this is your 'usband?"

Stella got out of her arm-chair and a shy smile broke on her lips as she listened with some confusion to the voluble old lady.

"Yes, that's Syd."

"Pleased to meet you," he said.

"And this is mine," said the old lady, with a little dig of the elbow in the direction of the tall white-haired man. "Mr. Penezzi. 'E's a count really, and I'm the Countess Penezzi by rights, but when we retired from the profession we dropped the title."

"Will you have a drink?" said Cotman.

"No, you 'ave one with us," said Mrs. Penezzi, sinking into an arm-chair. "Carlo, you order."

The barman came, and after some discussion three bottles of beer were ordered. Stella would not have anything.

"She never has anything till after the second show," explained Cotman.

Stella was slight and small, about twenty-six, with light brown hair, cut short and waved, and grey eyes. She had reddened her lips, but wore little rouge on her face. Her skin was pale. She was not very pretty, but she had a neat little face. She wore a very simple evening frock of white silk. The beer was brought and Mr. Penezzi, evidently not very talkative, took a long swig.

"What was your line?" asked Syd Cotman, politely.

Mrs. Penezzi gave him a rolling glance of her flashing, made-up eyes and turned to her husband.

"Tell 'em who I am, Carlo," she said.

"The 'uman cannon-ball," he announced.

deserves to be a success: it merits success □ **this is your 'usband**: this is your husband, isn't it?... I suppose

got out of: stood up from □ **shy** ≠ bold □ **broke**: came

confusion: embarrassment □ **voluble**: talkative; garrulous

Syd: abbreviation for *Sydney* (a fairly common London name)

pleased to meet you *(fam)*: how do you do? *(fml)*

mine: my husband □ **dig**: gesture

elbow = *coude* □ **tall** ≠ short □ **white-haired**: whose hair was white

'E's a count: He's a count

by rights: legally and/or morally □ **retired**: stopped working; went into retirement □ **dropped**: stopped using

will you have a drink?: what about something to drink?

you 'ave one with us: just let us pay (for the drinks) □ **sinking** *(sank, sunk)*: sitting down slowly, relaxing □ **you order** *(fam & emph)*: order; it's up to you to order

would not have anything: (said she) would not have anything (to drink); refused to drink anything

show: performance

slight: slim and light □ **light brown** ≠ dark brown

cut *(cut, cut, cut)*: short ≠ long □ **waved**: curled ≠ straight

lips = *lèvres* □ **little**: not much □ **skin** = *peau*

pretty: beautiful, good-looking □ **neat**: harmonious

wore *(wear, wore, worn)*: was dressed in □ **silk** = *soie*

evidently: clearly; obviously

talkative: voluble; conversational □ **swig**: drink

line: speciality

gave him a rolling glance: rolled her eyes at him □ **flashing**: dazzling, like flashes of lightning *(= éclairs)*

tell 'em: tell them

'uman: human □ **cannon-ball**: fired from a cannon

Mrs. Penezzi smiled brightly and with a quick, birdlike glance looked from one to the other. They stared at her in dismay.

"Flora," she said. "The 'uman cannon-ball."

She so obviously expected them to be impressed that they did not quite know what to do. Stella gave her Syd a puzzled look. He came to the rescue.

"It must have been before our time."

"Naturally it was before your time. Why, we retired from the profession definitely the year poor Queen Victoria died. It made quite a sensation when we did too. But you've 'eard of me, of course." She saw the blank look on their faces; her tone changed a little. "But I was the biggest draw in London. At the Old Aquarium, that was. All the swells came to see me. The Prince of Wales and I don't know who all. I was the talk of the town. Isn't that true, Carlo?"

"She crowded the Aquarium for a year."

"It was the most spectacular turn they'd ever 'ad there. Why, only a few years ago I went up and introduced meself to Lady de Bathe. Lily Langtry, you know. She used to live down 'ere. She remembered me perfectly. She told me she'd seen me ten times."

"What did you do?" asked Stella.

"I was fired out of a cannon. Believe me, it was a sensation. And after London I went all over the world with it. Yes, my dear, I'm an old woman now and I won't deny it. Seventy-eight Mr. Penezzi is and I shall never see seventy again, but I've 'ad me portrait on every 'oardin' in London. Lady de Bathe said to me: My dear, you was as celebrated as I was. But you know what the public is, give 'em a good thing and they go mad over it, only they want change; 'owever good it is, they get sick of it and then they won't

144

birdlike glance : a glance like a bird's (glance)

stared : looked intently

dismay : consternation; bewilderment

Flora : (I am) Flora

expected them to be impressed : was sure they would be impressed

quite know : (did not) know exactly □ **puzzled** : bewildered; baffled

came to the rescue : saved the situation

before our time : before we were born; before we were in the show business □ **retired** : stopped working; went into retirement

the year poor Queen Victoria died : the year (when)... died

quite a sensation : a real sensation, stir □ **you've 'eard of me** : you've heard (people talking) of me □ **blank** : expressionless

draw : attraction; it drew people to the theatre

at the old Aquarium, that was *(fam & emph)* : that was... Aquarium □ **swells** *(fam)* : famous people □ **who all** *(fam)* : who else, what other people □ **the talk of the town** : the person everybody was talking about in London □ **crowded** : filled (the Aquarium) full

turn : act, number, show

meself : myself (in a Cockney accent)

Lily Langtry : one of the Prince of Wales' most famous mistresses

remembered : recalled ≠ forgot

what did you do? : what was your act?

fired : ejected; you fire a gun; you also fire a bullet out of a gun

all over the world : everywhere; cf. all over Europe

I won't deny it : I admit it, I confess it

seventy-eight... is *(fam & emph)* : Mr. Penezzi is seventy-eight

'oardin' : hoarding i.e. place where advertisements are shown

you was *(fam)* : you were

give 'em : give them

go mad : go crazy, go wild (with enthusiasm)

'owever... : no matter how (good it is) □ **sick** : tired; bored (with)

go and see it any more. It'll 'appen to you, my dear, same as it 'appened to me. It comes to all of us. But Mr. Penezzi always 'ad 'is 'ead screwed on 'is shoulders the right way. Been in the business since 'e was so 'igh. Circus, you know. Ring-master. That's 'ow I first knew 'im. I was in a troupe of acrobacks. Trapeze act, you know. 'E's a fine-lookin' man now, but you should 'ave seen 'im then, in 'is Russian boots, and ridin' breeches, and a tight-fittin' coat with frogs all down the front of it, crackin' 'is long whip as 'is 'orses
10 galloped round the ring, the 'andsomest man I ever see in my life.''

Mr. Penezzi did not make any remark, but thoughtfully twisted his immense white moustache.

"Well, as I was tellin' you, 'e was never one to throw money about and when the agents couldn't get us bookin's any more 'e said, let's retire. An 'e was quite right, after 'avin' been the biggest star in London, we couldn't go back to circus work any more, I mean, Mr. Penezzi bein' a count really, 'e 'ad 'is dignity to think of, so we come down 'ere
20 and we bought a 'ouse and started a pension. It always 'ad been Mr. Penezzi's ambition to do something like that. Thirty-five years we been 'ere now. We 'aven't done so badly not until the last two or three years, and the slump came, though visitors are very different from what they was when we first started, the things they want, electric-light and runnin' water in their bedrooms and I don't know what all. Give them a card, Carlo. Mr. Penezzi does the cookin' 'imself, and if ever you want a real 'ome from 'ome, you'll know where to find it. I like professional people and we'd
30 'ave a rare lot to talk about, you and me, dearie. Once a professional always a professional, I say.''

146

it'll happen to you: you'll experience the same thing □ **same as** *(fam)*: just as

had his head screwed on his shoulders the right way: had a lot of common sense □ **been** = (he had) been □ **so high**: Mrs Penezzi must be indicating the height of a small boy □ **ring-master** = *Monsieur Loyal* □ **acrobacks** *(fam)* = acrobats

should 'ave seen 'im then: you ought to have seen him then

riding breeches: trousers worn on horseback □ **tight-fitting**: close to the body ≠ loose-fitting □ **frogs** = *brandebourgs* □ **crackin'**: making loud noises □ **whip** = *fouet* □ **'andsomest** *(fam)*: most handsome □ **see** *(fam)*: saw

thoughtfully: pensively

twisted: twirled i.e. curled (with his fingers)

'e was never one *(fam)*: he was never a man □ **to throw money about**: who would waste, squander money □ **bookin's** *(fam)*: bookings, reservations □ **an 'e** *(fam)*: and he □ **after 'avin' been** *(fam)*: after having been

I mean: to make my meaning clear; if you see what I mean

'e 'ad 'is dignity to think of: he had to think of his dignity

'a 'ouse: a house

thirty-five years we been 'ere now *(fam & emph)*: we've been here (for) thirty-five years now □ **we 'aven't done so badly** *(fam)*: we haven't done so badly; we've been fairly successful □ **slump**: economic depression □ **what they was** *(fam)*: what they were

the things they want *(excl)*: when I think of all they want!

runnin' water *(fam)*: running water i.e. water on tap □ **I don't know what all** *(fam)*: heaven knows what else □ **card**: i.e. hotel card

'ome from 'ome: home from home i.e. a place where you can feel at home; a homely place □ **professional people**: i.e. circus people

a rare lot *(fam)*: a great deal; a great many things □ **dearie** *(fam)*: (my) dear □ **once a professional**: if you have (once) been...

At that moment the head barman came back from his supper. He caught sight of Syd.

"Oh, Mr. Cotman, Mr. Espinel was looking for you, wants to see you particularly."

"Oh, where is he?"

"You'll find him around somewhere."

"We'll be going," said Mrs. Penezzi, getting up. "Come and 'ave lunch with us one day, will you? I'd like to show you my old photographs and me press cuttin's. Fancy you not 'avin' 'eard of the 'uman cannon-ball. Why, I was as well known as the Tower of London."

Mrs. Penezzi was not vexed at finding that these young people had never even heard of her. She was simply amused.

They bade one another good-bye, and Stella sank back again into her chair.

"I'll just finish my beer," said Syd, "and then I'll go and see what Paco wants. Will you stay here, ducky, or would you like to go to your dressing-room?"

Stella's hands were tightly clenched. She did not answer. Syd gave her a look and then quickly glanced away.

"Perfect riot, that old girl," he went on, in his hearty way. "Real figure of fun. I suppose it's true what she said. It's difficult to believe, I must say. Fancy 'er drawing all London, what, forty year ago? And the funny thing is her thinking anybody remembered. Seemed as though she simply couldn't understand us not having heard of her even."

He gave Stella another glance, from the corner of his eye so that she should not see he was looking at her, and he saw she was crying. He faltered. The tears were rolling down her pale face. She made no sound.

"What's the matter, darling?"

148

at that moment: just then □ **head**: (barman) in charge
caught sight of: happened to see
looking for you: searching for you; in search of you
particularly: specially, urgently

around: in the building; in the neighbourhood
we'll be going: we'll be getting off □ **come and 'ave lunch**: N.B. *and*
between *come/go* and the following verb, especially in orders or
invitations □ **will you?** = polite insistence □ **photographs**: taken by
a *photographer* i.e. with an interest in *photography* □ **'aving 'eard
of** = having heard (people talk) of
was not vexed: was not offended; did not take offence

bade *(bid, bade, bidden)* **one another good-bye** *(lit)*: said good-bye
to one another □ **sank** *(sink, sank, sunk)* **back**: slowly let her body
drop, fall
see what Paco wants: note the *invariable* order of words in this
indirect speech □ **ducky** *(fam)*: darling □ **dressing-room**: where
actors, etc., change, make themselves up, etc. □ **tightly**: firmly □
clenched: to make fists *(= poings)* □ **glanced away**: quickly turned
his eyes in another direction □ **riot** *(sl)*: joke; *(U)* fun
figure of fun: funny creature
fancy 'er drawing *(drew, drawn)*: (just) imagine her attracting
the funny thing is her thinking: the strange thing is that she thought
seemed as though: looked as if
understand us not having heard: understand (that) we had not heard
gave Stella another glance: glanced at Stella again □ **corner of his
eye**: furtively □ **so that she should not see**: in order for her not to
see □ **crying**: weeping; shedding tears □ **faltered**: hesitated □
rolling down: big round tears were running down
what's the matter: what's wrong? what's up?

149

"Syd, I can't do it again tonight," she sobbed.

"Why on earth not?"

"I'm afraid."

He took her hand.

"I know you better than that," he said. "You're the bravest little woman in the world. Have a brandy, that'll pull you together."

"No, that'd only make it worse."

"You can't disappoint your public like that."

10 "That filthy public. Swine who eat too much and drink too much. A pack of chattering fools with more money than they know what to do with. I can't stick them. What do they care if I risk my life?"

"Of course, it's the thrill they come for, there's no denying that," he replied uneasily. "But you know and I know, there's no risk, not if you keep your nerve."

"But I've lost my nerve, Syd. I shall kill myself."

She had raised her voice a little, and he looked round quickly at the barman. But the barman was reading the
20 *Éclaireur de Nice* and paying no attention.

"You don't know what it looks like from up there, the top of the ladder, when I look down at the tank. I give you my word, tonight I thought I was going to faint. I tell you I can't do it again tonight, you've got to get me out of it, Syd."

"If you funk it tonight it'll be worse tomorrow."

"No, it won't. It's having to do it twice kills me. The long wait and all that. You go and see Mr. Espinel and tell him I can't give two shows a night. It's more than my nerves'll stand."

30 "He'll never stand for that. The whole supper trade depends on you. It's only to see you they come in then at all."

150

do it again: do it a second time □ **sobbèd**: wept convulsively
why on earth *(excl)*: why in heaven's name
afraid: frightened, scared (to death)
took her hand: took her by the hand

in the world: after a superlative = *in* (before a place) □ **brandy**:
cognac or armagnac □ **pull you together**: revive you
worse: more frightening
disappoint your public: let your public down
filthy: despicable, contemptible □ **swine** *(fig)*: pigs
chattering: talking too much; chatterboxes □ **fools**: idiots
they know what to do with: know how to spend □ **stick**: stand, bear
□ **what do they care?**: how much do they worry? they couldn't care
less; they don't care, mind about me, about what happens to me
□ **thrill**: excitement (of danger) □ **there's no denying that**: no one
can deny that, say that is not true □ **uneasily**: not at ease
lost *(lose, lost, lost)* **my nerve**: I haven't the nerve, courage any more
□ **raised her voice a little**: spoken rather more loudly

paying *(paid, paid)* **no attention**: taking no notice
what it looks like: cf. order of words in a direct question; *what does
it look like?* □ **ladder** = *échelle* □ **tank** = *réservoir; bassin* □ **I give
you my word**: believe me □ **faint**: lose consciousness
you've got to get me out of it: you must save me from that
funk it *(sl)*: don't do it (out of fear or cowardice); back out
it's having to do it twice (that) kills me: zero relative
wait: period of waiting; suspense □ **go and see**: cf. p. 149, l. 7-8
two shows a night: two performances every evening
stand: bear, put up with
stand for that: tolerate that; agree to that □ **supper trade**: custom
from people coming to have supper (and watch the show) □ **it's
only... they come in** *(emph)*: they come in only to see you

151

He was silent for a moment. The tears still streamed down her pale little face, and he saw that she was quickly losing control of herself. He had felt for some days that something was up and he had been anxious. He had tried not to give her an opportunity to talk. He knew obscurely that it was better for her not to put into words what she felt. But he had been worried. For he loved her.

"Anyhow Espinel wants to see me," he said.

"What about?"

10 "I don't know. I'll tell him you can't give the show more than once a night and see what he says. Will you wait here?"

"No, I'll go along to the dressing-room."

Ten minutes later he found her there. He was in great spirits and his step was jaunty. He burst open the door.

"I've got grand news for you, honey. They're keeping us on next month at twice the money."

He sprang forward to take her in his arms and kiss her, but she pushed him away.

20 "Have I got to go on again tonight?"

"I'm afraid you must. I tried to make it only one show a night, but he wouldn't hear of it. He says it's quite essential you should do the supper turn. And after all, for double the money, it's worth it."

She flung herself down on the floor and this time burst into a storm of tears.

"I can't, Syd, I can't. I shall kill myself."

He sat down on the floor and raised her head and took her in his arms and petted her.

30 "Buck up, darling. You can't refuse a sum like that. Why, it'll keep us all the winter and we shan't have to do a thing.

streamed: flowed, ran in streams *(= ruisseaux)*

saw: realized

he had felt for some days: he had started feeling some days ago and he still felt (note the tense) □ **something was up**: there was sth wrong □ **anxious**: worried □ **opportunity**: occasion, chance

better for her not to put: (it was) better if she did not put

worried: anxious, concerned; full of anxiety

anyhow: in any case

what about: what (is it) about? what does it concern?

tell him (that) you can't: zero relative □ **give the show**: put on the turn, act

dressing-room = *loge d'artiste*

in great spirits: in a very happy mood

step: footstep □ **jaunty**: merry, carefree □ **burst open**: opened (the door) energetically □ **news** *(U)*: a piece of news □ **honey**: darling □ **keeping us on** ≠ sending us away □ **twice the money**: for two times as much money □ **sprang** *(spring, sprang, sprung)*: jumped, leaped

pushed him away: rejected his advance

have I got to go on: must I go on (the stage, the floor)

I'm afraid: here = "I'm sorry" (i.e. regret and not fear)

he wouldn't hear of it: he refused to listen to the idea □ **essential you should**: note *should* after the *adj* of coercion

it's worth it: it's worth while, worth the money, worth doing

flung *(fling, flung, flung)*: threw, cast □ **burst into a storm of tears** *(idiom)*: suddenly burst out crying, weeping, sobbing violently (like a storm = *orage*)

raised: lifted

petted: caressed, fondled (in order to calm her down)

buck up: don't lose heart; pull yourself together □ **a sum like that**: such a sum □ **winter**: i.e. the off season *(= morte saison)*

After all there are only four more days to the end of July and then it's only August."

"No, no, no. I'm frightened. I don't want to die, Syd. I love you."

"I know you do, darling, and I love you. Why, since we married I've never looked at another woman. We've never had money like this before and we shall never get it again. You know what these things are, we're a riot now, but we can't expect it to go on for ever. We've got to strike while
10 the iron's hot."

"D'you want me to die, Syd?"

"Don't talk so silly. Why, where should I be without you? You mustn't give way like this. You've got your self-respect to think of. You're famous all over the world."

"Like the human cannon-ball was," she cried with a laugh of fury.

"That damned old woman," he thought.

He knew that was the last straw. Bad luck, Stella taking it like that.

20 "That was an eye-opener to me," she went on. "What do they come and see me over and over again for? On the chance they'll see me kill myself. And a week after I'm dead they'll have forgotten even my name. That's what the public is. When I looked at that painted old hag I saw it all. Oh, Syd, I'm so miserable." She threw her arms round his neck and pressed her face to his. "Syd, it's no good, I can't do it again."

"Tonight, d'you mean? If you really feel like that about it, I'll tell Espinel you've had a fainting fit. I daresay it'll be
30 all right just for once."

"I don't mean tonight, I mean never."

She felt him stiffen a little.

four more days: another four days
it's only August: there's only August left
frightened: afraid, scared (to death)

you do (love me) □ **why** *(excl)*: after all; look here

money like this: this kind of money; this much money; as much money as this, as now □ **what these things are**: how things are □ **a riot**: a great success, draw; the talk of the town □ **strike while the iron's hot** *(idiom)*: take the opportunity while it lasts
d'you want me to die: N.B. proposition infinitive
don't talk so silly *(fam)*: don't say such stupid things
give way: give in; be discouraged □ **you've got your self-respect to think of**: you must think of your dignity □ **all over the world**: everywhere in the world (cf. all over Britain)
laugh of fury: furious peal of laughter
damned: bloody *(fam)*; cursed
the last straw *(idiom)*: the finishing blow □ **bad luck** *(U)*: a piece of ill luck
eye-opener: revelation; it opened my eyes □ **what... for**: why
on the chance: in case they are lucky enough
kill myself: get killed (accidentally)
forgotten *(forget, forgot, forgotten)* ≠ remembered, recalled
painted: made-up □ **hag**: ugly, often evil woman; witch
miserable: very sad, unhappy, depressed, dejected
it's no good: it's no use; it's useless (going on)

if you feel like that about it: if it makes you feel like that
a fainting fit: a serious faint = falling unconscious □ **daresay**: suppose, imagine □ **just for once**: one time only
I don't mean tonight: I'm not talking about tonight
stiffen ≠ relax

155

"Syd dear, don't think I'm being silly. It's not just today, it's been growing on me. I can't sleep at night thinking of it, and when I do drop off I see myself standing at the top of the ladder and looking down. Tonight I could hardly get up it, I was trembling so, and when you lit the flames and said go, something seemed to be holding me back. I didn't even know I'd jumped. My mind was a blank till I found myself on the platform and heard them clapping. Syd, if you
10 loved me you wouldn't want me to go through such torture."

He sighed. His own eyes were wet with tears. For he loved her devotedly.

"You know what it means," he said. "The old life. Marathons and all."

"Anything's better than this."

The old life. They both remembered it. Syd had been a dancing gigolo since he was eighteen, he was very good-looking in his dark Spanish way and full of life, old women and middle-aged women were glad to pay to dance with
20 him, and he was never out of work. He had drifted from England to the Continent and there he had stayed, going from hotel to hotel, to the Riviera in the winter, to watering-places in France in the summer. It wasn't a bad life they led, there were generally two or three of them together, the men, and they shared a room in cheap lodgings. They didn't have to get up till late and they only dressed in time to go to the hotel at twelve to dance with stout women who wanted to get their weight down. Then they were free till five, when they went to the hotel again and sat at a table, the three of
30 them together, keeping a sharp eye open for anyone who looked a likely client. They had their regular customers. At night they went to the restaurant and the house provided

156

I'm being silly: I'm having a *temporary* silly fit, period
it's been growing on me: it has been affecting me gradually
I do drop off *(emph)*: I eventually succeed in falling asleep
ladder = *échelle* □ **I could hardly get up it**: I could scarcely mount
it □ **trembling so**: shaking so much □ **lit** *(light, lit, lit)* **the flames**:
set fire to the petrol □ **seemed to be holding me back**: appeared to
be immobilizing me (N.B. *-ing* form on the infinitive after *seem* and
appear) □ **mind**: brain □ **a blank**: empty □ **clapping**: applauding,
clapping (their hands) □ **want me to go through**: wish me to endure
(N.B. *proposition infinitive*)
sighed: breathed out miserably; heaved a sigh □ **wet** ≠ dry
devotedly: he was devoted to her
what it means: what it implies; what the implications are
and all: and all that, *etcetera*
anything: anything else, whatever it is (is better...)

since he was eighteen: N.B. preterit in the phrase introduced by
since □ **good-looking**: handsome □ **full of life**: lively
middle-aged: neither really old nor quite young □ **glad**: content
out of work: unemployed; at a loss for a job □ **drifted**: wandered
without any real plan □ **stayed**: remained; settled
watering places: spas, such as Évian or Luchon, with thermal cures
it was not a bad life they led *(lead, led, led)*: they lived quite well
there were... two or three of them: note the English way of
expressing this □ **shared**: rented in common
late ≠ early □ **only dressed in time**: didn't dress until it was time
stout: corpulent
get their weight down: take off some kilos, some weight; reduce
the three of them: note the structure and cf. line 24
keeping a sharp eye open: on the look-out, on the watch
likely client: possible, potential, prospective customer
provided them with: gave them; supplied them with (a meal)

157

them with quite a decent meal. Between the courses they danced. It was good money. They generally got fifty or a hundred francs from anyone they danced with. Sometimes a rich woman, after dancing a good deal with one of them for two or three nights, would give him as much as a thousand francs. Sometimes a middle-aged woman would ask one to spend a night with her, and he would get two hundred and fifty francs for that. There was always the chance of a silly old fool losing her head, and then there
10 were platinum and sapphire rings, cigarette-cases, clothes, and a wrist-watch to be got. One of Syd's friends had married one of them, who was old enough to be his mother, but she gave him a car and money to gamble with, and they lived in a beautiful villa at Biarritz. Those were the good days when everybody had money to burn. The slump came and hit the gigolos hard. The hotels were empty, and the clients didn't seem to want to pay for the pleasure of dancing with a nice-looking young fellow. Often and often Syd passed a whole day without earning the price of a drink,
20 and more than once a fat old girl who weighed a ton had had the nerve to give him ten francs. His expenses didn't go down, for he had to be smartly dressed or the manager of the hotel made remarks, washing cost a packet, and you'd be surprised the amount of linen he needed; then shoes, those floors were terribly hard on shoes, and they had to look new. He had his room to pay for and his lunch.

It was then he met Stella. It was at Évian, and the season was disastrous. She was a swimming instructress. She was Australian, and a beautiful diver. She gave exhibitions every
30 morning and afternoon. At night she was engaged to dance at the hotel. They dined together at a little table in the restaurant apart from the guests, and when the band began

quite a decent: a fairly decent □ **meal** = *repas* □ **courses**: dishes
it was good money: it was a prosperous profession
anyone they danced with: anyone with whom they danced
a good deal: a lot; frequently
for: note *for* introducing duration
middle-aged: neither really young nor very old
spend *(spent, spent)* **a night**: sleep with her for a night
for that: in exchange for that; note *for* = exchange; cf. pay *for*
something □ **silly old fool**: stupid old idiot □ **losing her head**: here
= falling madly in love □ **rings**: to wear on your fingers
wrist-watch = *montre-bracelet* □ **to be got**: which could be
obtained; cf. there's a lot to be done = ... that must be done
to gamble with: (money) with which he could gamble; cf. line 11
the good days: the good times, the good period
money to burn: money (which) they could burn, waste, squander
hit the gigolos hard: was a blow, a catastrophe for the gigolos
didn't seem to want: seemed not to want □ **to pay for**: cf. line 8
nice-looking fellow *(fam)*: good-looking, handsome youg man □
often and often: very frequently □ **earning**: obtaining (for his work)
weighed a ton: was a ton in weight
had had the nerve *(fam)*: had been insolent enough □ **expenses**:
expenditure; overheads □ **go down**: diminish □ **smartly**: elegantly
□ **manager**: director □ **washing**: laundry □ **a packet** *(fam)*: a lot
amount: quantity □ **linen**: shirts etc. □ **shoes** = *chaussures*
were hard on shoes: wore shoes out quickly
he had his room to pay for: he was obliged to pay for his room
it was then he met Stella *(emph)*: that was when he met Stella
she was a swimming instructress: she taught people how to swim
a beautiful diver: she dived beautifully; she was very good at diving
engaged: taken on, hired
dined: had dinner
apart from the guests: separated from the customers

to play they danced together to induce the customers to come on to the floor. But often no one followed them and they danced by themselves. Neither of them got anything much in the way of paying partners. They fell in love with one another, and at the end of the season got married.

They had never regretted it. They had gone through hard times. Even though for business reasons (elderly ladies didn't so much like the idea of dancing with a married man when his wife was there) they concealed their marriage, it
10 was not so easy to get a hotel job for the pair of them, and Syd was far from being able to earn enough to keep Stella, even in the most modest pension, without working. The gigolo business had gone to pot. They went to Paris and learnt a dancing act, but the competition was fearful and cabaret engagements were very hard to get. Stella was a good ballroom dancer, but the rage was for acrobatics, and however much they practised she never managed to do anything startling. The public was sick of the apache turn. They were out of a job for weeks at a time. Syd's wrist-
20 watch, his gold cigarette-case, his platinum ring, all went up the spout. At last they found themselves in Nice reduced to such straits that Syd had to pawn his evening clothes. It was a catastrophe. They were forced to enter for the Marathon that an enterprising manager was starting. Twenty-four hours a day they danced, resting every hour for fifteen minutes. It was frightful. Their legs ached, their feet were numb. For long periods they were unconscious of what they were doing. They just kept time to the music, exerting themselves as little as possible. They made a little money,
30 people gave them sums of a hundred francs, or two hundred, to encourage them, and sometimes to attract

160

began to play : struck up □ **induce** : incite, encourage □ **customers** : clients; guests □ **floor** = *plancher, piste*

by themselves : on their own; all alone □ **neither of them** : neither the one nor the other □ **in the way of** : as

one another : each other □ **they got married** : they married

never regretted it : were never sorry for it □ **gone through hard times** : experienced difficult periods □ **elderly** : more than middle-aged and less than old □ **didn't so much like** : were not so eager about □ **concealed** : hid ≠ revealed

the pair of them : the two of them; cf. structure p. 157 1. 24

far from being able : quite unable to...; incapable of... □ **keep Stella... without working** : here = support Stella without her working, if Stella didn't work □ **had gone to pot** *(sl)* : was ruined

competition was fearful : the number of competitors was dreadful

engagements were hard to get : it was difficult to get jobs

rage : fashion; craze

however much they practised : no matter how much they practised; even by practising enormously □ **startling** : extraordinary □ **sick of** : tired of; fed up with □ **out of a job** : without work; unemployed □ **for weeks at a time** : for one week after another, for weeks on end □ **went up the spout** *(sl)* : disappeared; were sold off □ **reduced to such straits** : forced into such poverty □ **pawn** = *mettre en gage* □ **evening clothes** : formal dress □ **enter for** : be competitors for: put their names down for □ **starting up** : inaugurating; organizing □ **24 hours a day they danced** *(emph)* : they danced (for) 24 hours each day □ **frightful** : terrible □ **legs** = *jambes* □ **ached** : hurt; were sore □ **numb** : without feeling □ **unconscious** : unaware

kept time to : held the rhythm of □ **exerting themselves as little as possible** : using as little energy as they could

attract attention : draw *(drew, drawn)* notice

attention they roused themselves to give an exhibition dance. If the public was in a good humour this might bring in a decent sum. They grew terribly tired. On the eleventh day Stella fainted and had to give up. Syd went on by himself, moving, moving without pause, grotesquely, without a partner. That was the worst time they had ever had. It was the final degradation. It had left with them a recollection of horror and misery.

But it was then that Syd had his inspiration. It had come
10 to him while he was slowly going round the hall by himself. Stella always said she could dive in a saucer. It was just a trick.

"Funny how ideas come," he said afterwards. "Like a flash of lightning."

He suddenly remembered having seen a boy set fire to some petrol that had been spilt on the pavement, and the sudden blaze-up. For of course it was the flames on the water and the spectacular dive into them that had caught the public fancy. He stopped dancing there and then; he was
20 too excited to go on. He talked it over with Stella, and she was enthusiastic. He wrote to an agent who was a friend of his; everyone liked Syd, he was a nice little man, and the agent put up the money for the apparatus. He got them an engagement at a circus in Paris, and the turn was a success. They were made. Engagements followed here and there, Syd bought himself an entire outfit of new clothes, and the climax came when they got a booking for the summer casino on the coast. It was no exaggeration of Syd's when he said that Stella was a riot.

30   "All our troubles are over, old girl," he said fondly." We can put a bit by now for a rainy day, and when the

roused themselves: woke out of a daze; pulled themselves together
in a good humour: well-disposed; in a good mood □ **might bring
in**: could earn □ **terribly tired**: exhausted; worn out
fainted: lost consciousness □ **give up**: abandon (the competition)
□ **went on by himself**: continued, kept on dancing by himself, all
alone □ **worst time**: most trying experience; greatest ordeal
final degradation: last word; they had reached the bottom
misery: extreme unhappiness; wretchedness; hopelessness
inspiration: bright idea; brainwave
hall: large (often public) room; here = ballroom
saucer: what you put under your cup
trick: here = technique; special skill; knack
funny how ideas come: (it's) strange how you get ideas □ **a flash
of** *(U)* **lightning**: cf. a clap of thunder
set *(set, set)* **fire to**: light; set sth on fire
petrol = *essence* □ **spilt** *(spill, spilled/spilt, spilled/spilt)*: poured
accidentally □ **blaze-up**: conflagration
caught *(catch, caught, caught)* **the public fancy**: taken, captured,
fired the public's imagination □ **there and then**: immediately; on
the spot □ **talked it over**: discussed it in detail
a friend of his *(emph)*: one of his friends

put *(put, put, put)* **up**: provided, supplied □ **apparatus**: equipment
engagement: booking □ **turn**: act □ **a success**: successful
they were made: they had made it
outfit: set, ensemble
climax: culmination, crowning success □ **got a booking**: where
booked, engaged □ **no exaggeration of Syd's**: not one of Syd's
exaggerations □ **a riot**: a wild success; successful beyond their
wildest dreams □ **over**: finished; at an end □ **fondly**: lovingly
put a bit by: save a bit of money □ **for a rainy day**: in case we

public's sick of this I'll just think of something else."

And now, without warning, at the top of their boom, Stella wanted to chuck it. He didn't know what to say to her. It broke his heart to see her so unhappy. He loved her more now even than when he had married her. He loved her because of all they'd gone through together; after all, for five days once they'd had nothing to eat but a hunk of bread each and a glass of milk, and he loved her because she'd taken him out of all that; he had good clothes to wear again 10 and his three meals a day. He couldn't look at her; the anguish in her dear grey eyes was more than he could bear. Timidly she stretched out her hand and touched his. He gave a deep sigh.

"You know what it means, honey. Our connexion in the hotels has gone west, and the business is finished, anyway. What there is'll go to people younger than us. You know what these old women are as well as I do; it's a boy they want, and besides, I'm not tall enough really. It didn't matter so much when I was a kid. It's no good saying I don't 20 look my age because I do."

"Perhaps we can get into pictures."

He shrugged his shoulders. They'd tried that before when they were down and out.

"I wouldn't mind what I did. I'd serve in a shop."

"D'you think jobs can be had for the asking?"

She began to cry again.

"Don't, honey. It breaks my heart."

"We've got a bit put by."

"I know we have. Enough to last us six months. And then 30 it'll mean starvation. First popping the bits and pieces, and then the clothes'll have to go, same as they did before. And then dancing in lowdown joints for our supper and fifty

164

encounter bad weather i.e. hard economic times

without warning: quite unexpectedly □ **boom**: prosperity

chuck it *(sl)*: give it up; abandon everything □ **what to say**: what he could, should say □ **it broke his heart**: he was heart-broken

married her: (had) got married to her *(note preposition)*

gone through: endured

once: on one occasion □ **nothing... but**: nothing... except □ **hunk**: bit □ **she'd taken him out of all that**: she had freed him from all that

a day: every day *(distributive use of "a")*

anguish: anxiety, distress, dismay □ **bear**: stand; put up with

timidly: hardly daring; fearfully; timorously

gave a deep sigh: sighed deeply; breathed out sadly, miserably

means: implies □ **honey**: darling □ **connexion**: relationship, links

has gone west *(sl)*: has disappeared, vanished

what there is'll go: what remains (of the business) will go

what these old women are: how they are; what they are like □ **it's a boy they want** *(emph)*: what they want is a boy, a youth □ **it didn't matter so much**: it wasn't so important □ **a kid** *(fam)*: a boy, a youth □ **it's no good saying**: it's no use saying; it's useless saying □ **look my age**: look as old as I am really □ **get into pictures**: get an engagement in the cinema □ **shrugged**: gave a hopeless, depressed gesture of the shoulders □ **down and out** *(idiom)*: penniless; down to their last penny; *(fam)* on the rocks; *(fam)* (stoney) broke □ **I wouldn't mind what I did**: I wouldn't object to doing anything □ **for the asking**: simply by asking

we've got a bit put by: we've got a bit (of money) saved

I know we have... (a bit put by)

starvation: dying of hunger □ **popping** *(sl)*: pawning □ **bits and pieces**: one thing and then another; odds and ends

lowdown *(fam)*: doubtful, shady □ **joints** *(sl)*: cafés, night-clubs

francs a night. Out of a job for weeks together. And Marathons whenever we hear of one. And how long will the public stand for them?"

"I know you think I'm unreasonable, Syd."

He turned and looked at her now. There were tears in her eyes. He smiled, and the smile he gave her was charming and tender.

"No, I don't, ducky. I want to make you happy. After all, you're all I've got. I love you."

10 He took her in his arms and held her. He could feel the beating of her heart. If Stella felt like that about it, well, he must just make the best of it. After all, supposing she were killed? No, no, let her chuck it and be damned to the money. She made a little movement.

"What is it, honey?"

She released herself and stood up. She went over to the dressing-table.

"I expect it's about time for me to be getting ready," she said.

20 He started to his feet.

"You're not going to do a show tonight?"

"Tonight, and every night till I kill myself. What else is there? I know you're right, Syd. I can't go back to all that other, stinking rooms in fifth-rate hotels and not enough to eat. Oh, that Marathon. Why did you bring that up? Being tired and dirty for days at a time and then having to give up because flesh and blood just couldn't stand it. Perhaps I can go on another month and then there'll be enough to give you a chance of looking round."

30 "No, darling. I can't stand for that. Chuck it. We'll manage somehow. We starved before; we can starve again."

166

for weeks together: for whole weeks; for weeks on end, at a time
whenever: every time (when) □ **hear of one**: have news of one
stand for them: tolerate them; put up with them
unreasonable ≠ reasonable; sensible
there were tears in her eyes: she was on the verge of crying, weeping;
her eyes were brimming with tears □ **the smile (that) he gave her**:
N.B. *the zero relative*
ducky *(very fam)*: small duck; *fig* = darling □ **make you happy**:
N.B. *causative structure* = I will make (sure) you (are) happy
feel *(felt, felt)* **the beating of her heart**: feel how her heart was
beating □ **felt like that about it**: had that opinion of it
make the best of it *(idiom)*: make do (with it); put up with it □
supposing she were: note the subjunctive form *were* in a hypothesis;
what if she were □ **be damned to** *(excl)*: never mind; to hell with
honey *(fam)*: darling; *(fam)* ducky, sweetie-pie
released herself: freed herself; pulled herself free
dressing-table: where she kept her make-up, etc.
it's about time for me to be getting ready: it's almost time I was
getting prepared (note the preterit *was*)
started to his feet: stood up with a start, a sudden, convulsive
movement □ **you're not going to do** *(excl)*: you're surely not going
to do □ **what else is there**: what other solution is there?

stinking: nauseating; smelly; evil-smelling □ **fifth-rate**: lowdown
bring that up: mention that; refer to that; talk about that
dirty ≠ clean □ **give up**: abandon; *(fam)* throw in the sponge
flesh and blood: the body, the physique □ **stand it**: endure it
go on: keep on; continue
a chance: an opportunity □ **looking round**: prospecting
stand for that: tolerate, endure that □ **chuck it** *(sl)*: give it up
manage: make do □ **somehow**: in one way or another; by hook or
by crook □ **starved**: went without food; went hungry

She slipped out of her clothes, and for a moment stood naked but for her stockings, looking at herself in the glass. She gave her reflection a hard smile.

"I mustn't disappoint my public," she sniggered.

slipped... clothes : undressed with a few agile movements
naked : unclothed □ **but for :** except for □ **stockings** = *bas*
gave... a hard smile : smiled bitterly at her reflection (in the mirror)
disappoint : let down □ **sniggered :** laughed nervously; tensely

Grammaire au fil des nouvelles

Traduisez les phrases suivantes inspirées du texte (le premier chiffre renvoie à la page, les suivants aux lignes).

C'était lui qui avait pensé aux flammes (*emph = he was the one who...* ou bien : *it was...* 122 - 28).

C'était les flammes qui avaient fait que le numéro était devenu le grand succès qu'on connaissait (*emph + structure causative :* ici *= make + adjectif* ou *make + nom,* 122 - 29,30).

Stella plongeait dans un bassin du haut d'une échelle de 20 mètres (*remember :* 16 years old, 2 miles long, etc. 122 - 31).

Je n'hésite pas à vous dire qu'il ne va pas nous avoir aux mêmes conditions (commençons par : *I don't mind...* 124 - 13).

Tout ce que je demande c'est qu'elle ne se tue pas avant la fin du mois d'avril (après un superlatif, ou *every* et *all,* pas de *which* ou *who;* verbe coercitif + quel auxiliaire modal ? 126 - 18).

Elle s'arrêta assez longtemps pour qu'une représentante de la presse s'avançât avec son carnet de notes (idée de but, donc proposition infinitive introduite par *for* ? ou par Ø ? 126 - 29).

J'aime à me trouver tout près du bassin de manière à voir son visage (idée de but encore : ici employons *so that...* 128 - 25).

Il monta une douzaine de marches, de sorte qu'il se trouvait au même niveau que le bord du bassin (idée de conséquence ≠ but, donc ≠ infinitif, mais uniquement *so that,* 130 - 28).

C'est si vite passé qu'on n'en a pas vraiment pour son argent (it's hardly worth it! 134 - 16,17).

Je les connais depuis de nombreuses années. Cet homme en fait est un de mes compatriotes (temps du verbe ? préposition devant mesure de durée ? a compatriot of whose? 138 - 21,22).

Viens déjeuner chez nous un de ces jours (come + ? 148 - 7,8).

Elle ne pouvait pas comprendre que nous n'ayons même pas entendu parler d'elle (*understand + why* ou bien + *proposition complémentaire;* mais ≠ but, donc ≠ infinitif, 148 - 26,27).

On ne peut pas nier cela ! (you can't deny that... mais commençons par : *there's...* 150 - 14,15).

Le directeur ne voulait pas en entendre parler (152 - 22).

Il avait sa chambre à payer (to pay + ? 158 - 26).

Vocabulary

Voici approximativement 1 000 mots rencontrés dans les textes, suivis du sens qu'ils ont dans ceux-ci.

Les trois parties des verbes irréguliers sont données dans l'ordre alphabétique afin de faciliter la consultation. Les abréviations ne seront utilisées qu'en cas de nécessité, puisque la traduction seule suffira dans la plupart des cas pour indiquer s'il s'agit d'un nom, d'un adjectif, etc.

— A —

absent-minded distrait
accurate précis
ache faire mal
acknowledge reconnaître ; accepter
acquaintance connaissance
acquainted (become...) faire connaissance ; se lier
advice (*U*) conseil(s)
afraid (I'm) je regrette
ageing vieillissant
agent (commercial) représentant de commerce
agony douleur
ahead (go) y aller
aim but ; viser
airy reference remarque en passant
alight (set...) allumer
allow permettre
aloof hautain
alter transformer
amendment réforme
ammunition (*U*) munitions
annuity rente (viagère)
ant fourmi
anxious inquiet
apologize présenter des excuses
apology excuse
appearance apparence ; aspect
applause (*U*) applaudissement(s)
appliance appareil
appointment rendez-vous
arch avec coquetterie

argue discuter ; se disputer
argument discussion ; dispute
arm bras
artless innocent, candide
ascribe attribuer
ash cendre
ask demander ; inviter
assume supposer ; prendre
asylum asile
attempt tenter ; tentative
attend assister
attendant assistant
attire habillement
audience (*U*) spectateurs
aware conscient
awful épouvantable

— B —

backwater coin tranquille
bade *voir* bid
baggy qui fait poche
balance équilibre
bald chauve
baldness calvitie
ball boulet de canon
bally (*sl*) fameux
banc nu
bash (*sl*) fracasser
bath baignoire ; prendre un bain
bathe se baigner ; baignade
bathing cap bonnet de bain
bead perle (en verroterie)
bear porter ; supporter
beat (*beat, beat*) battre

beg mendier ; supplier
believe croire
bell cloche ; timbre ; sonnette
belong appartenir
bet (bet, bet) parier ; pari
bewildering désorientant ;
affolant
bid (bade, bidden) (lit) prier ;
ordonner
bill addition
bit (a...) un peu
blackmail chantage ; faire
chanter
blade of grass brin d'herbe
blameless immaculé ; sans
tache
bland suave
blank vide ; ébahi
blanket couverture
blaze éclat ; éblouissement
blaze-up flambée
blew voir blow
blow (blew, blown) souffler
blow coup
blow up faire sauter
bluff direct ; jovial
body corps
bold hardi ; audacieux
book réserver ; engager
bookshelves rayonnages
bore ennuyer ; personne,
chose ennuyeuse
bore through traverser
borrow emprunter
bother s'inquiéter
bottom fond
bound to en partance pour

bound (be...to) être obligé
de
bow s'incliner ; saluer ; salut
brain(s) cerveau ; intelligence
brandy cognac ; armagnac
break out éclater
bright vif (couleurs)
brilliance partie éclairée
brim bord (chapeau ; verre)
bring (brought, brought)
porter
bring about provoquer
bring himself se résoudre
bring home faire compren-
dre
bring up élever ; faire état de
brisk énergique
broad large
broker agent de change
brought voir bring
brushed peigné
brute égoïste
buck up (fam) reprendre
courage
building bâtiment
bulge être distendu
burden fardeau
burly bien charpenté
burst (burst, burst) éclater
burst into tears éclater en
sanglots
bury enterrer
business (U) affaire(s)
but sauf ; excepté
but for à l'exception de
by avant ; dès
by (oneself) tout seul

— C —

cab fiacre ; taxi

calling vocation ; métier ; profession

canvas toile

capital ville capitale

capital (*U*) capital, capitaux

car voiture

care se soucier

case affaire

case (in...) de peur

cash argent liquide ; encaisser

casual fait en passant

cautious prudent

censer encensoir

century siècle

chance hasard ; occasion

chance (on the...) dans l'espoir

change one's mind changer d'avis

chat bavarder ; conversation

chatter bavarder ; bavardage

cheat tricher ; escroquerie

cheek joue

cheerful optimiste ; réjoui

cheese fromage

chicken poulet

childhood enfance

chin menton

chip jeton

chit note ; addition

chorus chœur

chuck up (*fam*) abandonner ; plaquer

chuckle glousser ; gloussement

cicada cigale

civil poli, courtois

claim prétendre ; revendiquer

clam huître

clean-shaven glabre

clench (hand, fist) serrer (les poings)

climax point culminant ; apogée

climb grimper, monter

cloak cape

cloakroom vestiaire

clock horloge ; pendule

clock-tower clocher

close intime

commission (on...) contre un pourcentage

commonly ordinairement

commonplace banal

conceal dissimuler

confide (in) se confier (à)

congratulate féliciter

consulting room cabinet de médecin

convenient commode

conversation conversation ; pourparler

convict condamner

cooking cuisine

cool frais ; fraîcheur

cost coût

cost (*cost, cost*) coûter

couple couple ; 2 ou 3

course plat (repas)

course direction

course of life cours de la vie

cowshed étable

crack (whip) faire claquer (un fouet)

cracked fêlé

cradle berceau

craft métier ; activité

craftsman artisan

creased froissé

crisp frisé

crowd foule

crowded bondé

curl boucle

cursory bref

customer client

cut (*cut, cut*) couper

cut décolleté

cut up attristé

cutting coupure

cuttlefish seiche

cynic (*n*) cynique

cynical (*adj*) cynique

cynicism (*n*) cynisme

cross-eyed qui louche

— D —

dare oser

daresay (I...) (je) suppose, m'imagine

dart darder

deal (*dealt, dealt*) distribuer

deal with résoudre

deal (a good...) (*adv*) bien, beaucoup

debt dette

definitely définitivement

deliberate contrôlé ; étudié

delight ravir ; ravissement

deny nier

deputy...barman second barman

deserve mériter

desk table de travail

determined décidé, résolu

devise inventer ; créer

devoted dévoué

die mourir ; mourir d'envie

dig coup de coude ; pointe (de méchanceté)

dim vague

dinner-jacket smoking

dip plonger ; plongeon

disappoint décevoir

disapprove désapprouver

disapproval désapprobation

discreditable scandaleux

discuss (a problem) discuter (d'un problème)

disinclination réticence

dissolute dissolu

distraught défait ; hagard

dive plonger

diver plongeur

doings faits et gestes

double-breasted suit costume croisé

drank *voir* drink

draught courant d'air

draw (*drew, drawn*) tirer ; attirer ; dessiner

draw a breath respirer profondément

draw (*n*) attraction

dress (*U*) habillement

dress (a...) robe

dress (s') habiller

dressing-gown robe de chambre

dressing-room loge d'artiste

drift errer

drink (*drank, drunk*) boire ; boisson

drip s'égoutter

drive (*drove, driven*) conduire ; pousser

drop laisser tomber ; renoncer

drop off s'assoupir

drove *voir* drive

drum tambour

drunk *voir* drink

drunk (*adj*) ivre, saoul

dry sec ; sous le régime de la Prohibition

ducky (*fam*) mon petit chou

dud fiasco

dull ennuyeux

dusty poussiéreux

duty devoir

dye teindre ; teinture

— E —

eager ardent

earn (one's living) gagner (sa vie)

else autrement

else (who, what...) qui, quoi d'autre

embassy ambassade

emergency urgence

empty vide ; (se) vider

energetic énergique

engaged (to) fiancé(e) (avec)

engineer ingénieur

engraving gravure

enjoy (oneself) s'amuser

enlarge upon développer ; s'étendre sur

entail impliquer

enter for (s')inscrire

entertain distraire ; recevoir ; donner des réceptions

entice attirer, tenter

entitle donner le droit

entitled (be...) avoir droit

erect droit

evening-dress tenue de soirée

exhilarating grisant ; enivrant

expect s'attendre à

expenses frais

expensive cher

experiment expérience ; tentative

explain expliquer

exquisite exquis ; raffiné

eyebrow sourcil

eyelid paupière

eye-opener (*fam*) révélation

— F —

factory usine

fail échouer ; manquer

faint s'évanouir

fair juste

faithful fidèle

176

fake tricherie
fall (*fell, fallen*) tomber ; être dupe
falter hésiter
fancy envie ; avoir envie de
fancy imaginer ; imagination ; goût
far éloigné
far left tout à fait à gauche
fashion mode
fashion (out of...) démodé
fashionable élégant ; à la mode
fate destin
feast fête ; festin
feat exploit
feather boa boa
feature trait
feel (*felt, felt*) sentir
feel like avoir envie
feelings (*plur*) sensibilité(s)
fell *voir* fall
fellow (*fam*) type ; semblable
fellow-countryman compatriote
felt *voir* feel
fetch aller chercher
fifth-rate de 3e ordre
fig figue
figure corps ; proportions ; silhouette
fill remplir
filthy sale ; crasseux
fine beau
finger doigt
fire tirer ; projeter
fire (set...to) mettre le feu à ; allumer

firing party peloton d'exécution
firing squad peloton d'exécution
first name prénom
fist poing
fit crise
fit out équiper
flaming enflammé
flash (of lightning) éclair
flash across traverser (l'esprit)
flashing brillant
flatter flatter
flesh chair
flesh and blood (more than...can stand) insupportable
fleshy charnu
flew *voir* fly
flick chiquenaude ; lancer en l'air
flick (...a coin) jouer à pile ou face
flight (of steps) volée de marches
fling (*flung, flung*) jeter
floor plancher ; piste de danse
flounder patauger
fluently couramment
flung *voir* fling
fly (*flew, flown*) (...into a fury) s'emporter
fly fiacre
food nourriture
fool idiot
foot (*plur* feet) pied ; 33cm
footpath sentier

forehead front
foresee prévoir
forgive pardonner
forth (and so...) et ainsi de suite
fortnight 15 jours
framed encadré
free libre ; gratuit
fresh frais ; nouveau
frock robe légère
frog brandebourg
frost givre ; gel
frown froncer les sourcils
fun amusement
funk (*sl*) se dégonfler
funny drôle, amusant ; bizarre
furnish meubler

— G —

gait démarche ; allure
gamble jouer (de l'argent)
gambler joueur
gaol prison
garment vêtement
gasp avoir le souffle coupé
gather réunir ; rassembler ; s'assembler
gaunt décharné
gave *voir* give
genteel distingué
gentle doux
genuine authentique ; sérieux
get (*got, got*) obtenir
get out sortir

get up se lever
get-up attirail
giddiness étourderie
gilt-edged securities placements de père de famille
ginger ale limonade
give (*gave, given*) donner
given *voir* give
give up abandonner ; renoncer
glad heureux ; satisfait
glance coup d'œil ; lancer un coup d'œil
gloom tristesse ; mélancolie
go (*went, gone*) aller
go into examiner
go west (*sl*) être fichu
gone *voir* go
good time (have a) s'amuser
gossip bavarder ; commère ; (*U*) bavardage(s)
got *voir* get
got (have...) avoir, posséder
grape raisin
grasshopper sauterelle ; cigale
grave tombe
great (the...) les grands de ce monde
grim sinistre
grin large sourire ; grimace
grove verger ; bois
grudge regretter ; accorder à contrecœur
guess deviner
guest invité(e)
gutter caniveau

— H —

hag sorcière
haggard pâle ; défait
half-humorous à demi amusé
hamper entraver
hand main ; tendre ; donner de la main à la main
handsome beau ; élégant
hanky-panky (*fam*) entourloupette
happen avoir lieu ; se passer
happen (to do) faire par hasard
harbour port ; bassin
hard on presque
hard-working travailleur
hardly à peine
hardy résistant ; vivace
hare lièvre
harmless innocent ; inoffensif
hazard risque
hazardous dangereux
head tête
head barman premier barman
hear (*heard, heard*) entendre
hear of entendre parler de
heart cœur
hearty cordial
heaven ciel
heavy lourd ; grand (buveur, fumeur)
heel talon
height hauteur ; taille
held *voir* hold
help aider ; aide
help (not...doing) ne pouvoir s'empêcher de faire
high-flown déclamatoire
hinder empêcher ; entraver
hint faire allusion ; insinuer
hip hanche
hoarding panneau publicitaire
hold (*held, held*) tenir ; prise
hole trou
honey miel ; (*fig*) chéri(e)
host hôte ≠ guest
hover planer
however cependant
however (+ *adj* ou *adv*) pour si...que ; quelque...que
huge énorme
hungry (feel...) avoir faim
hunk gros morceau
hurt (*hurt, hurt*) faire mal ; blesser

— I —

idle oisif
ill-fitting mal ajusté
ill-read illettré
impress impressionner
inclined (be...) être enclin ; avoir envie
income revenu
increase augmenter
indefatigable infatigable
induce inciter
indulge in se permettre (un luxe)
industry travail

infamous infâme
infirmary hôpital
infirmity faiblesse
ingenious ingénieux
ingenuity ingéniosité
ingenuous ingénu; naïf
ingenuousness ingénuité; naïveté
inhabit habiter
inhabited habité
inn auberge
insane fou
insensible inconscient
intent attentif
interview entrevue; interview
introduce présenter
invaluable inestimable

— J —

jabber jacasser
jaunty guilleret
jewellery (*U*) bijoux
join se joindre à
join in participer à
joint boîte (de nuit); gargotte
joke plaisanterie; histoire drôle
jolly heureux
journey voyage

— K —

keep entretenir; garder
keep (+ *-ing*) continuer
kid *(Am)* enfant
kind(ly) gentil
king roi
knave valet; scélérat
knock frapper
knock down terrasser

— L —

lack manquer; manque
lacking (*adj*) déficient
ladder échelle
larder garde-manger
late tard; feu, décédé
laughter (*U*) rire
lawyer homme de loi
lay-down (have a...) s'étendre
lead (*led, led*) mener; conduire
lean se pencher
lean maigre
leap sauter
learn apprendre
least moins; moindre
led *voir* lead
lemon citron
lend (*lent, lent*) prêter
level niveau
levy lever (impôt; armée)
life vie; *voir* living
light clair (couleurs); léger
light lumière

likely susceptible ; possible ; éventuel

line spécialité

lined ridé

linen linge (de corps)

lip lèvre

listen (to) écouter

livelihood gagne-pain

living (earn one's...) gagner sa vie

living (cost of...) coût de la vie

living (standard of...) niveau de vie

loan emprunt ; prêt

look for chercher

look forward to (+ -ing) espérer ; tarder

look out (one's own...) sa propre responsabilité

loose: lâche, détaché ; flasque

loosen détacher

lose (*lost, lost*) perdre

loud fort (bruits)

low grave ; doux (voix)

lowdown de bas étage

lower baisser

lumber bric-à-brac

lunch déjeuner

lurk rôder

luxurious luxueux

make (*made, made*) faire

make a living gagner sa vie

manage réussir

mankind humanité

mat (of hair) masse

match allumette

meal repas

mean vouloir dire ; dire sérieusement ; dire vrai ; avoir l'intention

meaning sens

means (*sing* & *plur*) moyen(s)

mercy mansuétude

merely simplement

middle-aged d'un certain âge

mind esprit ; intelligence

mind (*v*) (don't...) accepter

miserable malheureux

misery malheur

miss manquer

monk moine

moral moralité (de l'histoire)

morale (*n*) moral

morals (*plur*) morale ; moralité

move into déménager

mug (*sl*) bonne poire

murder meurtre

murderer assassin

mutter murmurer ; marmonner

— M —

maim estropier

mainland continent

— N —

narrow étroit
nasty malveillant ; méchant
neat net, précis ; rangé ;
   mignon ; élégant
neck cou
neighbour voisin
nerve (keep one's...) garder
   la tête froide
neutral neutre
next door tout près
nice-looking beau
nod dire bonjour ; dire oui ;
   opiner (de la tête)
notice remarquer
notwithstanding malgré ;
   néanmoins
novel roman

— O —

oblige obliger ; rendre service
oblique détourné
obviously de toute évidence
occasionally quelquefois
occur arriver ; se produire
occur (it...s to me) il me
   vient à l'idée
odd étrange ; disparate
oleander laurier-rose
only seulement ; unique
order ordonner
outfit jeu ; ensemble
outsider (*n*) marginal
outstretched tendu en avant

oven four
over fini
over and over sans cesse
overlook surplomber ; ne
   pas faire attention
overwhelming écrasant ;
   extrême
owe devoir
owner propriétaire

— P —

packet (*sl*) grosse somme
pagan païen
pair couple ; deux
part with se séparer de
party groupe ; réception
pass oneself off for se faire
   passer pour
pass through traverser
patch tache
patience (play...) faire des
   réussites
pattern modèle ; schéma
pawn mettre en gage
peasant paysan
pebble caillou ; galet
peeled (keep...eyes...) garder l'œil ouvert
peg pieu
pension pension de famille
pension off mettre à la
   retraite
people (my...) mes amis ;
   mes parents
perform accomplir

performance numéro; séance (de spectacle); représentation

pet caresser

philander (*lit*) flirter; courir les femmes

pink rose

placid calme; tranquille

point (make a...) mettre un point d'honneur

poke coup de poing

pop (*sl*) mettre au clou

portly corpulent

pot (go to...) (*fam*) être fichu

pour verser

practise pratiquer

prepared prêt

presently bientôt; tout à l'heure

prevalent généralement admis

prim pincé; guindé

progress se dérouler

prominent éminent

properly comme il convient

propose (se) proposer

proprietor (landed...) propriétaire terrien

prosecute poursuivre en justice

prove prouver; s'avérer

provide fournir

provided pourvu que

pugnacious combatif; querelleur

pull oneself together se ressaisir

punctual à l'heure

punctually à l'heure; à temps

punish punir

put (*put, put*) mettre

put by mettre de côté

puzzled perplexe; étonné

— Q —

qualm scrupule; remords

quay quai

quest quête; recherche

quiet tranquille; silencieux

quite assez; complètement

— R —

race fréquenter les champs de course

rage grande mode

rainy day (*fig*) jours plus sombres

raise lever; élever (la voix)

ramshackle décrépit

ran *voir* run

rattling bruyant

raven corbeau

reach atteindre

ready prêt

recall (se) remémorer

recover récupérer; guérir

regardless nonobstant

relation parent; relation

relative parent

release lâcher

relief soulagement
relieve soulager
remain rester
remind rappeler
rent loyer
repine regretter
report bruit (d'un coup de revolver)
representative délégué; typique
rescue secourir; secours
resign donner sa démission
resignation résignation; démission
resigned résigné
respects hommages
respite répit
retire se retirer; prendre sa retraite
retirement retraite
reward récompense; récompenser
riding breeches culotte de cheval
rig up équiper
rights (by...) de droit
ring sonner; sonnerie; coup de fil; bague; piste (de cirque)
ring-master Monsieur Loyal
riot (*sl*) succès fou; tabac; phénomène
roast rôtir; rôti
rogue gredin
roll rouler; roulement
roll-top desk bureau à cylindre
rotten pourri; désagréable
rough peu raffiné

rub frotter
ruffian scélérat
rule règle; règlement
rumour bruit (qui court)
run (*ran, run*) courir
run série
run across rencontre par hasard
run through dilapider
running water eau courante
ruthless impitoyable; inexorable

— S —

sacrifice sacrifice; sacrifier
sail in entrer majestueusement
same même
sand sable
sang *voir* sing
sank *voir* sink
saucer soucoupe
saunter flâner
sausage saucisse
scamper décamper
scanty minuscule
scapegrace vaurien, bon à rien
scar cicatrice
scare effrayer; alerte
scheme projet
scornful dédaigneux
scoundrel gredin; escroc
scrap (*fam*) bagarre
scrap-iron ferraille
scream crier

scream (be a...) (*fam*) être drôle

screwed on (head...) tête sur les épaules

scrunch crisser ; crissement

scruple scrupule

search rechercher ; recherche

seek (*sought, sought*) chercher ; s'efforcer

self-confidence assurance

self-respect amour-propre

sense sens ; bon sens

sensible sensé ; raisonnable

serried (...throng) foule serrée

set (*set, set*) **about** se mettre à ; entreprendre

settle régler

settle down s'installer ; s'assagir

shabby élimé

shake (*shook shaken*) secouer ; ébranler

shake (...head) dire non de la tête

sharp aigu ; brusque

sheep mouton

sheep (black...) brebis galeuse

shell obus

shift transférer

shine (*shone, shone*) briller

shingle (*U*) galets

shipwrecked naufragé

shirt chemise

shiver frisson ; frissonner

shone *voir* shine

shook *voir* shake

shore rivage

short court ; courtaud ; petit

shoulder épaule

shrug hausser les épaules

shy timide

sick (...of) lassé de

sick-making écœurant

sickly écœurant

sigh soupir ; soupirer

sight vision ; spectacle

sight (catch...of) apercevoir

silk soie

sing (*sang, sung*) chanter

sink (*sank, sunk*) couler ; baisser ; s'effondrer ; s'affaler

sit (*sat, sat*) **down** s'asseoir

sitting (be...) être assis

sitting séance

skin peau

sky ciel

sleek gominé

slender mince ; svelte

slide glisser

slight menu

slightly légèrement

slim mince ; svelte

slip glisser

slip out of enlever prestement

slow lent

slump dépression économique

smart élégant

smithereens (blow to...) faire éclater en mille morceaux

smoke (*U*) fumée(s)

snigger ricaner ; ricanement

sob sanglot ; sangloter

sober sobre ; à jeun

somehow d'une manière ou d'une autre

sorry triste

sorry (be...) regretter

sorry (be...for) prendre en pitié

sort trier, classer

sought voir seek

soul âme

sovereign pièce d'or d'une valeur d'une livre sterling

space espace

spend (*spent, spent*) dépenser ; passer

spill verser

spin (*spun, spun*) tisser ; tournoyer

spin (...a coin) jouer à pile ou face

spine colonne vertébrale

spirits (*plur*) humeur

spout (up the...) (*sl*) être bazardé

spread (*spread, spread*) se répandre

spring (*sprang, sprung*) bondir ; s'élancer ; jaillir

spun *voir* spin

spurt jaillir

squad (firing...) peloton d'exécution

squeamish facilement dégoûté ; délicat

squint strabisme ; de travers

stack (...cards) tricher en battant les cartes

staff personnel

stage scène (de théâtre)

stake enjeu ; mise

stand (*stood, stood*) se tenir ; supporter

stand for supporter ; accepter

stand out se dresser

star étoile

stare regarder fixement

start départ ; début ; partir ; commencer

startle effaroucher

starve mourir de faim

staunch fidèle

stay hauban

steady calmer ; détendre

steal (*stole, stolen*) voler ; glisser (un regard)

steamer bateau à vapeur

stick (can't...) ne pouvoir supporter

stiffen raidir

stink puer ; puanteur

stir remuer ; émouvoir

stir mouvement ; brouhaha

stole, stolen *voir* steal

store stock ; provision

storm orage ; tempête ; accès

stout corpulent

straight out directement

straightforward droit ; intègre ; direct

straits (*plur*) situation difficile

stranger inconnu

straw paille ; (*fig*) dernière goutte

streak of lightning éclair

stream ruisseau ; ruisseler

stretch étendre

stretch out étendre ; envoyer au tapis

strike (*struck, struck*) frapper ; se mettre en grève

strike up (*orchestre*) attaquer (un air)

stroll flâner

struck *voir* strike

strum improviser

stunt tour spectaculaire ; acrobatie

subside s'éteindre

subtle subtil

suit costume ; convenir

suitable approprié ; qui peut convenir

sulky maussade

sum somme

sum up faire le tour (d'une question, d'une personne) ; résumer

summary résumé ; sommaire

sung *voir* sing

sunk *voir* sink

sunset coucher de soleil

support soutenir ; subvenir aux besoins de

surmise supposer ; supposition

survey (*lit*) regarder

suspect soupçonner

sweep down descendre majestueusement

swell (*sl*) rupin

swig gorgée

swine (*sing & plur*) porc(s)

sympathize (with) compatir (avec) ; comprendre

sympathy compréhension ; compassion ; condoléances

— T —

table table de jeu

take (*took, taken*) prendre

take in observer ; enregistrer ; duper

talk parler ; (sujet de) conversation

talk sth over discuter de qqch.

talkative bavard

tall grand ; haut

tank réservoir ; bassin

tap tapoter ; tape

tear larme

tempt tenter

tenant locataire

term condition

that (at...) qui plus est ; de plus

thence de là

thin maigre

think (*thought, thought*) penser

though bien que

thought *voir* think

thought pensée

thoughtful pensif

thoughtless inconsidéré

thread his way se frayer un chemin ; se faufiler
threw *voir* throw
thrift énonomie
throat gorge
throaty guttural
throng foule
throw (*threw, thrown*) jeter
thumb pouce
thus ainsi
tight serré ; ivre ; soûl
tight-fitting bien ajusté
tighten resserrer
tightly fort (serrer)
time (have a good...) s'amuser
time (keep...) être au rythme, en mesure
tiny minuscule
tittle-tattle (*U*) bavardage(s) ; scandale(s)
toe orteil
tone down adoucir
took *voir* take
toss down avaler (d'un trait)
tout (*pej*) racoleur
tower tour ; se dresser
trade commerce ; métier
train former
training formation
tram-car tramway
trick tour ; truquage ; coup (à prendre)
trifle bagatelle
trifle (a...) un peu
trifling de peu d'importance
trouble souci ; ennui ; (se) donner du mal
trout truite

true vrai ; réel
trunks (*plur*) maillot de bain (pour homme)
truth vérité
tumbledown en ruine
turn numéro
turn (do a good...) rendre service
turn out s'avérer
twice 2 fois
twiddle frémissement
twist rouler ; caresser

— U —

ugly laid
uneasy mal à l'aise ; gêné
unfailing infaillible ; constant
unfortunate malheureux
unless à moins que
unsatisfactory peu satisfaisant
untidy inélégant ; mal coiffé
unwilling peu enthousiaste, peu enclin
unwillingly contre son gré
up to (be...) être sous la responsabilité de
upper supérieur
upright tout droit
useful utile
useless inutile

verge (on the of...) sur le point de

vine vigne

vineyard vigne

vivid vif (couleurs)

voyage traversée ; voyage en mer

waddle se dandiner

wage (war) faire la guerre

waist taille

waisted cintré

war guerre

warn prévenir ; avertir

wary méfiant

wash laver

waste gaspiller ; perdre (son temps)

waste (*U*) déchet(s)

watering-place ville thermale

wave faire signe de la main ; onduler

waved ondulé

wavy ondulé

weak faible

weakness faiblesse ; faible

wealth richesse ; fortune

wear (*wore, worn*) porter ; user

whisper chuchoter ; murmurer ; parler à voix basse

whole (on the...) dans l'ensemble

why pourquoi ; mais alors ; en fait

wide large

widow veuve

wife femme (mariée) ; épouse

wig perruque

wild sauvage ; féroce ; fou

willing prêt

willing (be...) accepter

willingly volontiers

wind serpenter

wine vin

wipe out éliminer

withdraw (*withdrew, withdrawn*) (se) retirer

woodshed cabane

word mot ; parole (d'honneur)

wore *voir* wear

workhouse hospice (des pauvres)

world monde

worn *voir* wear

worn (*adj*) usé

worried inquiet

worse pire, pis

worst le pire

worth valeur

worth (be...) valoir

worth (get one's money's...) en avoir pour son argent

worthless (*adj*) bon à rien

worthy digne ; honorable

wound blessure

wrap envelopper

wrath (*lit*) colère

wrinkle ride

wrinkled ridé

— Y —

youth jeunes ; jeune homme ; jeunesse

Composition réalisée par COMPOFAC - PARIS

IMPRIMÉ EN FRANCE PAR BRODARD ET TAUPIN
Usine de La Flèche (Sarthe).
LIBRAIRIE GÉNÉRALE FRANÇAISE - 6, rue Pierre-Sarrazin - 75006 Paris.
ISBN : 2 - 253 - 05037 - 7